OLD   LEIGH
A Pictorial History

OLD LEIGH

A Pictorial History

by

JOHN F. BUNDOCK

PHILLIMORE

1978

Published by
PHILLIMORE & CO. LTD.
Shopwyke Hall, Chichester, Sussex

Reprinted 1985, 1994

© Text and illustrations John F. Bundock, 1978

ISBN 0 85033 281 2

Dedicated to all the old Leigh families

Printed and bound in Great Britain by
BIDDLES LTD
Guildford and King's Lynn

CONTENTS

ILLUSTRATIONS

I PREFACE

The phrase 'the changing face of Britain' is in common usage nowadays, and everyone knows what it means. The face of Britain has always been changing to some extent, but more in the last few generations than ever before.

No place has changed more in this time than the town of Leigh. Before the railway came in the 1850s Leigh consisted of the High Street by the waterside, a few dwellings on the slopes above, particularly on Leigh Hill, the Church with the Rectory, Leigh House and the manor house, Leigh Hall. There was a small pottery on the eastern boundary, partly in the neighbouring parish of Prittlewell. The rest was farm land with seven small farm houses.

Now we see the old town in a state of more or less dereliction while the former agricultural land has provided sites for new houses accommodating a population of tens of thousands. Some may lament these changes; others will regard them as inevitable—part of progress.

Fortunately some pictorial matter has survived to give us an idea of what parts of the former Leigh looked like. The coming of photography coincided with the big changes in Leigh, and we must be thankful that so many photographs of old Leigh and its people have come down to us.

The destruction of old Leigh took place in two phases: (*a*) with the coming of the railway in the 1850s when a strip of demolition passed through the town from one end to the other. Many old places were destroyed of which we have no record save on maps; (*b*) the demolition of properties in more recent years because they were not up to the required standards of modern housing. There has been with the authorities an obsession for a 'road to the west', which started with the idea of continuing Westcliff front to Leigh and the development of the High Street as its western terminus. Then the policy was changed so that the 'road to the west' was to be another entrance and exit to the borough running parallel with the railway. Either policy involved the destruction of the High Street, so the Corporation has bought up and demolished quite an appreciable amount of property as it has come on to the market.

Only comparatively recently has the public conscience been aroused over the destruction of old buildings and an urge has arisen to conserve what is old. Appropriate legislation has been brought in and now preservation orders are placed on old and worthy buildings. Had this existed a century ago old Leigh would be looking quite different now.

The Report of the Royal Commission on Historical Monuments (Essex, Volume IV) 1923, listed seven Leigh buildings other than the church. Now only two of them remain—The Crooked Billet and the old Custom House.

Buildings alone do not make a town. People play an essential part. Therefore a book that publishes pictures of old Leigh buildings must also include representatives of the folk who lived in them.

This book is not a history of Leigh though it has strong historical associations. No real complete history of Leigh has yet been written, perhaps because we are lacking in adequate records, or maybe because no one has yet applied himself to the task of seeking records in obscure and unexpected places. Benton made an invaluable contribution in his chapter on Leigh in *The History of the Rochford Hundred*. J. H. Burrows gave adequate treatment of Leigh in his local history. More recently the late Alderman H. N. Bride gave us *Old Leigh* which is a real mine of information on the subject.

The aim of the present book is to give illustrations of buildings and scenes of Old Leigh which either no longer exist or which have been altered out of recognition. In addition there are pictures of old Leigh people almost all of whom belong to the 19th century. That which still exists and can be readily seen still, even though old and worthy, has, with just one or two special exceptions, not been included. It is assumed that it is not necessary to print what can be seen in a walk down the High Street or round the church.

The author is greatly indebted to the kind and willing co-operation of many people. Although many of the pictures have come from his own collection a great number have been lent for the purposes of the book. The author is grateful to all who helped in this way: The Victoria and Albert Museum for permission to portray the Chester Steeple Cup; the National Maritime Museum for the reproduction of the portrait of Admiral Nicholas Haddock; Major T. R. Mordaunt-Hare, M.C., and the National Portrait Gallery for the picture of Bishop Hare; the Beecroft Art Gallery and Southend Central Library (Mr. F. J. M. Easton, Librarian); the Chelmsford District Library (Mr. S. M. Jarvis, Librarian). Mr. Donald Fraser has kindly allowed me to reproduce some etchings of Leigh in his possession made by his great grandfather, Rev. Edmund Worlledge, who was curate of Leigh 1843-44. These have never been published before.

Others who have co-operated are Brigadier C. E. F. Turner, C.B.E., D.S.O. (portraits of the Salmon family), Mr. N. L. S. King, Mr. L. G. Arnold, Mrs. J. V. Banner, Mrs. Mary Bartlett, Mr. Stuart Brewer and Mrs. Brewer, Mr. Frank Cotgrove, Mr. P. Cotgrove, Miss M. F. Foster, The Trustees of New Road Methodist Church and Rev. Arthur Freeman, Mr. R. J. Hankin, Mr. L. G. Harvey, Mr. H. J. L. Johnson, Mr. R. G. Johnson, Mr. J. H. W. Lacy and Profile Publications, The Salvation Army and Mr. R. Little, Mrs. C. Meddle, Councillor A. V. Mussett, J.P. and Mrs. Mussett, J.P., Mr. C. Osborne, Mrs. M. M. Padgham, Mrs. J. K. Payne, Mr. Peter Powell, Mrs. A. E. Read, Mrs. Frank Rushbrook, Mrs. B. Rose, Mrs. J. M. Saul, Mrs. I. K. Thornton, Miss Rosemary Thornton and Mr. E. B. Thorp.

Many of the above have also supplied me with valuable information and helped to identify people and scenes. In addition to the above I acknowledge help from Captain E. F. Pizey, D.S.O., O.B.E., R.N. and Mrs. P. M. Jenkins of the Naval Secretary's Department; Dr. W. J. Petchey and Mr. A. C. Edwards (Essex Record Office) for helping to identify the Bank House stained glass, Councillor Vera Smith, J.P., Rev. Raymond Smith for permission to photograph objects in St. Clement's, Mr. John Bridge for putting his boat at our disposal to examine and photograph old quays, and to him and his wife Angela for much miscellaneous help and information; Stephen Dunlop of Southend High School for Boys for making a picture of Eden Lodge from a decayed photograph; Mr. Hervey Benham, Mrs. F. H. Boulton, Mr. Percy and Mr. Louis Cotgrove, Mr. and Mrs. Ernest Cotgrove, Mr. 'Ruffy' Johnson, Mr. E. Little, Mrs. S. Pitt-Stanley, Mr. H. H. Tomlin and Mrs. J. K. Payne.

I cordially acknowledge the kindness and help that I received from the staffs of Essex Record Office and the Southend and Chelmsford Libraries.

A work of this sort is entirely dependent upon the photographers' skill, and I am grateful in the extreme to all that Mr. Nixon Payne of Chelmsford has done for me, and also in some cases Mr. Richardson of Leigh.

JOHN F. BUNDOCK

BIBLIOGRAPHY

Benton, Philip, *History of Rochford Hundred* (Vol. I).
Burrows, J. W., *Southend-on-Sea and District*.
Bridge, H. N., *Old Leigh*.
Essex Review, vols. I, II and III.
Murie, James, *Report & MSS in Southend Library*.
King, H. W., *MSS in Essex Record Office*.
Hearth Tax Rolls in Essex Record Office.
Tithe Map and Instrument of Apportionment (Leigh) in Essex Record Office.
Facsimile of the Domesday Book.
Report of Royal Commission on Historical Monuments (Essex) vol. IV.
Map of Leigh in 1873, published by Leigh Representative Committee, 1964.
Dictionary of National Biography.
Burke, *Landed Gentry*.
Johnson, S. F., *Michael Tomlin (1814-1903)*.
Benham, Hervey, *Once upon a Tide*.
Marsh, Edgar, *Inshore Craft of Britain*, vol. I.
Profile Publications, No. 27, *Tilbury Tanks*.
Southend Standard, Files in 19th century.
Southend Graphic, Files from 1903.

II LEIGH IN THE DOMESDAY BOOK

THIS IS THE FIRST KNOWN WRITTEN REFERENCE TO LEIGH

Translation

Hundred of Rochford. Legra held by R. in demesne, was held by 1 freeman as a manor and as 1 hide. Always 2 villeins and 2 bordars, and 1 plough on the demesne and half a plough belonging to the men, and 5 bordars by the water who hold no land. Pasture for 100 sheep. Then 1 rouncey, 5 cows, 5 calves, 100 sheep. Now 2 rounceys, 4 cows, 5 calves, 103 sheep. It was then worth 40 shillings, now 100.

Notes.
1. Legra was the name for Leigh in those days.
2. R. is an abbreviation of Ranulfus (Latin for Ranulf)
3. A rouncey is a horse.
4. The Domesday Book was compiled in A.D. 1085 and 1086.

III MAP OF LEIGH IN 1845

The sketch map of Leigh in 1845 is based on the survey map of the parish that accompanied the Tithe Award. It was presented in 1847 so it must be assumed that the rather detailed survey was made some time before this, say in 1845. We have included only the built up area of the parish; from just beyond Billet Lane in the west to the bend in Leigh Hill in the east, from the water front in the south to about Rectory Grove in the north.

Two rows of cottages and Belton Farm are therefore omitted to the west of the map, while Leigh Hall, Oak Farm and the Pottery are the only buildings omitted to the east in Hall Road. There was nothing further in the north until you reach London Road, and then there were only four sets of buildings on the London Road from the Hadleigh boundary to the Prittlewell boundary, namely Leigh Heath Farm, Leigh Park Farm, Lapwater Hall and the Elm. Then north of the London Road there were Belfairs Farm, Gowles Farm and Brickhouse Farm which had to be omitted. In short, the rest of Leigh parish outside the map was agricultural land or woodland with the few exceptions we have noted.

One of the most interesting features of the map is that it was made before the railway came to mutilate the old town. The positions where it entered and left the map are marked 'R', and it passed through the Market Place marked '7' on the map.

The following buildings or sites have been numbered: 1. St. Clement's Church; 1. The old Rectory, now the Public Library; 3. Leigh House; 4. Lady Sparrow's School; 5. Eden Lodge; 6. The Ship Inn; 7. The Market Place; 8. The King's Head Inn; 9. The Bell Wharf; 10. Match Corner House; 11. The Strand; 12. The Peter Boat Inn; 13. The original Methodist Meeting House; 14. The Crooked Billet Inn; 15. Site of the Haddocks' family house.

Dwelling houses and buildings of a permanent nature have been marked in black, but sheds and the like have been marked in outline only. In many cases one building marked in black was a group of several cottages or tenements.

The reader will observe that in 1845 the following roads did not exist; New Road, Leigh Park Road and Rectory Grove. Elm Road has been so described on the map, but although it existed then as a country road the author has no proof that it was called Elm Road at that time. The road called on the map Church Hill Lane no longer exists and it must not be confused with the present Church Hill.

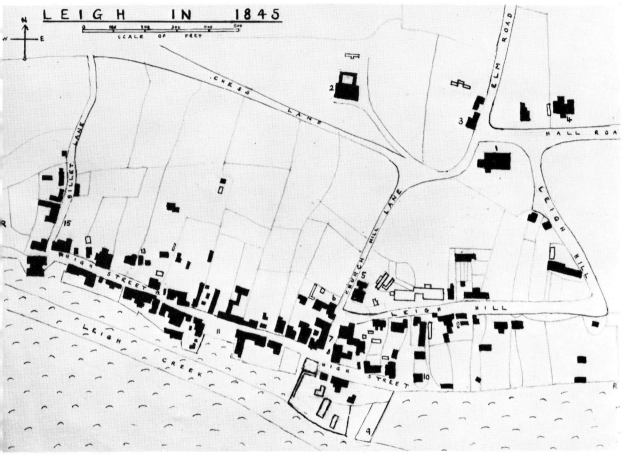

2. Map of Leigh in 1845.

IV THE HIGH STREET

For many centuries until recent times the High Street was the principal, and virtually the only, concentration of dwellings in the parish. The street began, as it does now, at the Bell Wharf, though actually the wharf itself was not made until the early part of the last century. The first house on the north side (No. 10 on the map) had the intriguing name of Match Corner House. It was destroyed to make room for the railway or siding.

A narrow road went up from the High Street to Leigh Hill at this point. It is still easy to trace at the Leigh Hill end. The original Bell Inn was on the east side of this little road. It was another victim of the railway, but it was replaced by another licensed house of the same name. The large building in Leigh Hill is still there but no longer licensed.

From the eastern end of the High Street there were houses, shops and inns continuously to beyond the Crooked Billet, except on the shore side where the Strand and other openings gave access to the sea, and on the land side where roads or narrow alleys went northwards.

When the High Street was the principal road in the parish there were shops in it of all descriptions which could supply the ordinary needs of the inhabitants. There were butchers, bakers, grocers, clothiers and bootmakers. Some of them looked for business other than from the inhabitants as they advertised outside their shops 'Shipping Supplied'.[1] There were ships' chandlers and industries such as boat building, and blacksmiths supplying the needs of fishing boats and barges. A good deal of merchandise came into or went from the wharves by barges. On one wharf there was a lime kiln.

Every day large quantities of fish were being landed and sent to market so that Leigh High Street was a hive of industry.

The principal entry to the High Street was at the foot of Leigh Hill. When the railway came in 1855 this entry was blocked by a level crossing with gates. In the early days when trains were few, this caused little inconvenience, but when the train service became more frequent and commuter passengers vastly increased the gates were often closed for long periods. Finally, when electrification came in 1961 the road was permanently blocked, so what had been the thoroughfare into old Leigh for perhaps more than a thousand years ceased to be. The writer cannot recall that anyone made more than a formal protest at this violation of our forefathers' rights.

Before the coming of the railway this spot (no. 7 on the map) was centre of the little town and it was known as the Market Place, though of course Leigh never had a market in the strict sense of the term. At the north west corner was The Ship Inn (on the same site as at present) (No. 6 on the map). At the south east corner was the King's Head Inn (No. 8), pictures of which have survived, but the size of the building was reduced by the railway.

It is easy to trace the old High Street because it follows the same course as formerly. Most of the old buildings have gone and their sites have been left derelict or replaced by other structures. The author has done his utmost to portray as much of the old High Street in pictures, limited by the material available.

The turning leading into Billet Lane has now been permanently blocked, but another side turning, near the Peter Boat, though blocked by the railway has a footbridge as a substitute. The road leading from the Bell Wharf to Leigh Hill became a level crossing at first. Litigation followed the railway company's attempt to close it. Later it was replaced by a footbridge (from which some of our photographs were taken) but this has now been removed.

The High Street, in spite of its present state of dereliction, is our visible reminder of many generations—forefathers of many Leigh people—who lived and worked, and had their joys and their sorrows in this little town by the sea.

Note
1. See picture 13.

3. The eastern end of the High Street: view from the Bell Wharf looking up the hill. Before the coming of the railway you would have looked up a narrow road where you can now see the foot-bridge in the picture. There were dwellings each side of the road and on the right was the old Bell Inn. The railway and the coal and goods yard altered all this. Then later the 'up' platform of the old Leigh station was built after this picture was taken. There was strong local objection, led by the late Canon Walker King, the Rector, to the closure of this road to make room for the railway. Here you see the beach where the Leigh children played. The breakwaters farther on had not yet been constructed, nor was the Cinder Path in existence.

4. View from the footbridge in the last picture looking west. On the extreme left is the High Street with old cottages, the Smack Inn and Juniper's shop. The two large buildings left of the centre are the King's Head. The white part of the building was much larger before some was taken down to make room for the railway. The dark part was a house in which a Mr. Wilkin lived (Tithe Award No. 32) until it was incorporated into the King's Head to enlarge it after its loss of a large part. Note the level crossing gates at the extreme right. The train is standing in the down station. In those days the 'up' station was opposite to it. Note the very old buildings on the right, all of which have since been demolished. (Plate 167 is a picture of an original locomotive on our railway)

5. The High Street from the Bell Wharf end. The fishermen are standing round the well sunk by Lady Olivia Sparrow, Lady of the Manor, in 1836 to improve Leigh's poor water supply (Benton, *History of Rochford Hundred* Vol. I pp. 397-400. This well is said there to be 249 feet deep). Note the old weather-boarded cottages on the left. It was in one of these that Mr. Cotgrove and his wife had a fish shop in later years. By the time this picture was taken the new 'up' station to the right of the picture had been built.

6. The same site in the 1920s. The well and pump are gone and Mr. and Mrs. Cotgrove have extended their premises to cater for the increasing holiday trade. Now all this is an open space and car park.

7.   The King's Head (No. 8 on the map). This was demolished to make way for the 'up' station as it was until the entirely new station was opened in 1933 at the bottom of Belton Way. The old station building is now the headquarters of Leigh Sailing Club. The shops on the right are a late addition. There was an open site here adjoining the Victoria (or Phoenix) Wharf in the 1845 map.

8.   The High Street looking west (about 1884). The original entrance to the old railway station is on the right, up the flight of steps. Next to it is Mr. Edric Brewer's grocer's shop. On the left is the Smack (formerly on the other side of the road). Beyond is the early Tudor building known to a later generation as Joe Juniper's fish shop. In the picture it is F. Barrett's butcher's shop. No buildings in this picture except the rebuilt Smack remain.

9. (*above*) The High Street again from a slightly different angle. On the right, farther on are three old buildings. One is a very old house called 'Long Clerke's Shipman' (Bride, Old Leigh, p. 40. However Benton p. 333 suggests this house was on a site just south of Leigh House.) Beyond is the Old Custom House which still stands. The first named was once the Waterman's Arms. Also in this range of buildings is Cooks Place, (Royal Commission on Historical Monuments, Vol. IV p. 84(a) where the house is described) where Dr. Cook lived when he is said to have given hospitality to John Wesley during at least one of his visits in the 18th century, and in which he preached. The house has been destroyed.

10. (*right*) The Grocer's shop and Post Office about 1875. Thomas Busby had this shop early in the 19th century, followed by his son and other members of the family. The picture shows Mr. Harry Busby and his three sisters, Mary (right), Annie and Ellen (the children). The two at the back are other members of the Busby family. Annie eventually married Edric Brewer and so the business came to him and his name is seen over the shop in the previous picture.

11.   The Level Crossing. This was probably in the early 1920s. The view is facing north and the picture is taken from the High Street and looks across to Leigh Hill. The 'down' station is on the left and the 'up' station on the right. A good deal of heavy horse traffic went up the hill from the wharves where it had been unloaded from barges. The cart load of bricks is typical. A vintage taxi can be seen. Evidently trains had kept the gates closed a long while and pedestrians did not feel inclined to use the footbridge on the left but out of sight in this picture.

12.   The Level Crossing from the Bell Bridge. The new 'up' platform and booking office were built on the site of the King's Head and yard. The picture was taken looking west from the bridge. The 'down' platform was on the right beyond the crossing gates.

13. High Street in the Twenties. Very little had changed just here except that the old station had gone from this point and a footbridge provided. There was still a good deal of horse traffic and as Leigh Hill (sometimes called Horse Hill) was so steep extra horses were harnessed for the pull up the hill and they were unharnessed at the top of the hill and came back light. They were kept by the bridge to await the next load.

14. Juniper's Shop. Before the destruction of most of the High Street this was one of the best known of all the buildings. (R.C.H.M. Vol. IV p. 84(a) for description and p. XXXIV (8) for illustration.) It was really one dwelling with the adjoining house, but had been divided at some time. This happened to almost all the larger houses possessed by prosperous Elizabethan mariners when they died out. The date 1589 was carved on a stone found in the walls. The shop front was added when it became first a butcher's and then a fishmonger's shop. Originally the upper storey projected over the ground floor for the whole length of the building. There is an old tradition that John Constable stayed here while he painted his famous picture of Hadleigh Castle. There is no documentary evidence of this and the lengthy volumes of his letters do not mention his stay. The house was destroyed in 1952.

15. Houses on the Strand. Leigh Strand was always an important landing place for the old mariners, and many had dwellings very near the Strand. Deeds, wills and the manor documents confirm this. On the east side of the Strand was a **large** house which had come in recent times to be divided into four tenements. 'Inside the building is an original staircase with a central newel and the roof retains a queen-post truss with cambered tie beams, curved wind-braces and octagonal queen-posts'. (R.C.H.M. Vol. IV p. 84(a).) The present writer witnessed its demolition during or just after World War II. Under the high chimney to the left of the picture was the original Tudor brick fireplace. This was demolished with all the rest. The house was the residence for some time of Richard Chester, Master of Trinity House in 1615. (See section on the Mariners)

16. The House of Richard Chester. We repeat this picture, very similar to the last, to show the position of the house in relation to the water. The craft moored near the shore is a bawley belonging to the days of sail before engines were introduced. It is probably awaiting repair at the boat builders just behind the house. On the Strand was another well sunk by Lady Olivia Sparrow to augment Leigh's scanty water supply. This well was sunk in 1832.

17. The Old Peter Boat Inn. The original building dated back at least to the 17th century, and it was owned in that century and the next by several generations of the Osborne family including three successive members of the family all called John. The building was burnt down in 1892 in a disastrous fire which damaged other buildings in the locality. As the Leigh people found it impossible to put out the fire, Herbert Brewer, whose family lived nearby, rode a horse bare-backed all the way to Southend to call the Southend Fire Brigade to help. They had just commissioned a new steam-driven fire engine called 'The Alert' and the Peter Boat fire was the first time it went into action. A contemporary account in the Southend Standard says the Southend Fire Brigade arrived in fifteen minutes. Presumably this did not include Brewer's wild-west dash to Southend. In those days there was only open country between Leigh and Southend. Note the very old cottages on both sides of the High Street. The picture was taken facing east.

18. The High Street looking west from the Peter Boat. The inn was rebuilt after the fire. The range of buildings on the right were the least interesting part of the High Street. The original Methodist Meeting House, built in 1811 or shortly after, was approached towards the end of the picture on the right, but it is not visible in the picture.

19. The High Street looking east. The United Brethren was a beer house on the corner of the alley going northward. It was almost opposite the Peter Boat.

20. Brewers the Butchers—about 1875. This range of houses and shops was immediately west of the Peter Boat—the site now being part of a car park. Here are Mr. and Mrs. Brewer and their four sons, Frederick, Edric, Herbert and Arthur. Mr. B. S. Brewer was for a time a Church-warden, and both he and his wife took a prominent part in Leigh affairs.

21. Farther down the High Street, looking east. A century ago Leigh High Street was thickly populated and there were always plenty of children to be seen. The boot maker's shop belonged to one of an old and well known Leigh family—John Emery. The buckets on the right belong to folk waiting to get water from the Conduit—one of the few supplies of fresh water in Leigh. The Conduit House has recently been restored. It is just out of sight in this picture.

22. The Billet Wharf—east side. The old cottages (R.C.H.M., Vol. IV p. 84(a), (6) for a description of these houses), timber framed and weather boarded, were 16th or 17th century. They have now been demolished. The cottage at the rear on the right is not really old and it is still there. The west side of the wharf is occupied by Osbornes' cockle shed—though once it was the site of a dwelling.

23. The Salmon family house. This dwelling was in the High Street east of the Crooked Billet. When it was demolished in 1912 it was known as Osborne House, the name being derived from previous owners. It was one of the houses occupied by members of the Salmon family who were Leigh mariners from the 15th to the 17th century. There is a fine monument to Robert Salmon (see picture 103), 1641, Master of Trinity House, on the north wall of the church and brasses to other members of the family. Their house illustrated here has been described as of date 1600, but the timber framework and the lath and plaster or even wattle and daub of the walls is consistent with an earlier date. The triangular section of the roof suggests there was once a gable here that had become ruinous and was removed.

24. The end of the High Street, looking east. This is taken from the water colour drawing by G. A. Fripp, R.W.S., in the Beecroft Art Gallery. It is dated 1852 and the author believes by comparing it with maps and prints that it is a fairly accurate representation of that part of Leigh as it was then. Gilmans is on the left, and Jone Bayliss (by then turned into a number of tenements) is on the right. All this is now pulled down. A fisherman is seen mending what might well be a peter net. Fishermen mended their nets within living memory on that grass patch. The net may be hanging on the last relic of the 'pale'. The boats are peter boats or pinkies. The bawley had not been evolved yet. These boats are smaller than bawleys.

HIGH STREET, LEIGH-ON-SEA.

W.WEST
6

25. The west end of the High Street. First we notice the Crooked Billet, the only part of the picture that is still there, and one of the two secular buildings in Leigh mentioned by the Royal Commission in 1923 that have survived. As it still remains we shall not describe it here. Beyond it was the end of Billet Lane. A level crossing was provided when the railway came, but that has now gone. The building beyond was a beer house called the Coal Hole when the picture was made in the last century. It had seen much better days, and H. W. King in his unpublished manuscripts gives a detailed description of the property and its former owners. (These manuscripts are now in the Essex Record Office.) The house was originally called Gilmans-at-the-Pale, the pale being the protective fence at the west end of Leigh. King describes it as being 'perhaps the most ancient house remaining in the town and may be assigned to the reign of Queen Elizabeth (I) if not older, as the fireplace is of the Tudor period. It had an overhanging upper storey until quite recently when it was faced with red bricks'. The earliest owner that King found was John Flower. It passed in 1634 to John Bundocke and remained with him and his descendants for a century. The Allison family had the property for a long while, but by then it had been divided into three or four tenements. The railway company bought the property, severed the garden and orchard for their own use and sold the rest. Since World War II it has been acquired by Southend Corporation and demolished. On the opposite side of the High Street there was the gasworks, the gas container dominating the scene. Formerly there was an old house called Jone Bayliss here with its own water front and wharf. This also belonged to the Bundocke family in the 17th century.

V BILLET LANE

Originally the lane began in the High Street immediately to the west of the Billet and proceeded due north to the top of the hill unimpeded. When the railway came a level crossing was provided where the railway crossed the lane, but this was closed when the railway was electrified. New Road did not exist until after the railway came, and recent development has also altered the lower end of the lane so that it now begins higher up. As the parish workhouse was on the east side of the lane the old Leigh people called it 'Work'us' Lane. At the top of the lane bridle ways went in three directions: 1. West, parallel with the present Marine Parade; 2. North west following the present upper end of Hadleigh Road; 3. East into Chess Lane, leading to the church, but later into Rectory Grove, as at present. The map published by the Leigh Representative Committee in 1964, (based on the 1874 Ordnance Survey) will help the reader to understand these paths and the geography of old Leigh generally at that date.

26.   The south end of Billet Lane. This picture was taken at the railway level crossing before the turn of the century. It is at the intersection of Billet Lane with New Road. Bride mentions that on the right 'was an old timber house, later refronted with brick and ultimately turned into a beerhouse under the name of The Old Billet. The house was sold by Sir Richard Haddock in 1707. It appears to have been not only Sir Richard's birthplace but also that of his son Admiral Nicholas Haddock, and of other members of that famous naval family. When it ceased to be a beerhouse the licence was transferred to the Coal Hole which almost adjoined the Crooked Billet. (Bride, Old Leigh p. 42) The Haddocks' house is not marked on the 1845 Tithe map, so we can assume that it was demolished before that date. There is plenty of space for the house at the place where it must have been sited—marked 15 on the map. Note in the picture the young lady with a yoke and buckets. She was evidently on her way to the conduit in the High Street, on the other side of the railway, to draw a supply of water for the household.

27. The Work House. The aged and infirm were cared for here unless they had relatives who would take them in. This was in the days before Boards of Guardians and the Unions were instituted. When the Rochford Union was established the old work-house was used as a private dwelling house. It is the house on the right in the last picture. Later it was weather boarded and done up, but how grim and dreary it must always have been so devoid of light. Thank God we treat the old and destitute in a more Christian way nowadays.

28. The Third Methodist Church in Leigh. John Wesley paid his first visit to Leigh in 1748, and other visits in 1749, 1750, 1755 and finally 1756. In these early days of Methodism the severance from the Church of England, its sacraments and services did not take place. None the less those who followed the Method met together for fellowship and worship. Exclusive places of worship and separation from the Church of England came at a later stage. However in Leigh in 1819 (Benton, p. 395) the Methodists produced their own meeting house at a place marked No. 13 on the map. This was demolished in 1854 to make room for the railway and another meeting place was used in the High Street. (The minister at this time was Joseph Gutick.) However in 1879 a larger building was needed so the new chapel in New Road was built. This is the one illustrated in our picture. It was replaced by a new church in 1932. In 1897, as the population up the hill was growing, a hall for worship was provided in Elm Road, and in 1904 the present Wesley Church. In these days Mr. John Osborne was the Methodists' prime benefactor.

29. Pittington House. Mr. William Foster, who was landlord of the King's Head and a coal merchant, built this house for his own occupation in the early 1850s. It was well sited, facing the sea, and high enough up the hill to have a view of the sea unimpeded. It was east of Billet Lane and was approached from New Road. It had extensive gardens. The house has now been pulled down and the site developed

30. Spring head of the old conduit. (Benton, pp. 397–400.) In the Rectory grove, on the north side, not far from Billet Lane, this stone can still be seen, though it has several times been removed short distances from its original position. There was a rather copious spring, probably now under Rectory Grove, from which water was piped to the old town. It was stored in cisterns on the way down, one of which can still be seen in Leigh Park Road. The final tap from which inhabitants used to draw their water was east of the Billet wharf on the south side of the High Street. The tap house has recently been restored by the local Chapter of Architects as their contribution to Conservation Year 1975. They are to be greatly commended for their initiative after the tap house had been so long neglected. If readers have not known all about this they should first find the stone and then go down to the High Street to see the newly restored tap house. The old Leigh people called it (phonetically) the 'cundit'.

VI LEIGH HILL

The hill began at the Market place—later the level crossing—and proceeded, as now, up to the church in an irregular direction to avoid steep gradients. It was otherwise known as Horse Hill (because it was the only entry for horse-drawn vehicles into the High Street), and some can remember it also being called Turnpike Hill. Next to the High Street it had the largest number of dwellings in it, though, except at one spot, there was no congestion of tenements like you found in the High Street. The upper arm of the road had no dwellings on the east side until the later part of the 19th century and the west side had two houses and a row of cottages dating from perhaps the 18th century.

A rough road[1] proceeded up the slope from the east side of The Ship Inn in an almost northerly direction, and it turned east at the top towards the west gate of the churchyard. This was the usual road to the church from the High Street. When the National School was built in 1847 Church Hill was made and the old road to the church was closed. This caused popular protest because Church Hill was too steep to carry corpses up for burial,[2] and they were forced thereby to use the longer route via Leigh Hill.

The geography of that part of Leigh has changed considerably since the Tithe map survey, and this will also be evident from some of our pictures.

Notes
1. Benton says it was kept clean by depositing cockle shells from Canvey on it. (P. 377)
2. Ibid. pp. 377-8.

31. Old house by the level crossing. This old building with second storey and dormer window survived the coming of the railway. For a time it was a house agent's office. It was demolished at the early part of this century. The new footbridge which has replaced the level crossing now covers the site. In ancient times this house faced the Market Place. Note the end of the old 'up' station, and in particular the shrimp pads in the fish store waiting to be transported by train to Fenchurch Street for Billingsgate Market.

32. The view up Leigh Hill. The view on the left has changed very little, but every building on the right hand side has been demolished. All the shops on that side were old. The first was Mr. J. H. Johnson's grocery, bakery and off-licence; next was Mr. Stivey's newsagency, then Mr. (Wap) Robinson's fish shop. The site is now occupied by the footbridge and a car park.

33. The Ship Inn before rebuilding. Originally there was a 'mansion house' belonging to Thomas Stephens on this site. (Bride, Old Leigh, pp. 39-40) The central part of the building in the picture may well have been the mansion house, or part of it, judging by the chimney and the tiles. In this case it is assumed that the front and the west side were added at a later date. The whole building has since been entirely rebuilt.

34.   Eden Lodge. This rather quaint house stood on the north side of Leigh Hill, and it was east of the junction between Leigh Park Road and Leigh Hill. It seems that it was a Tudor house with an 18th century front super-imposed. Richard Chester, either the one who was Master of Trinity House in 1615 and at one time lived in the house in the Strand, or one of his family, lived at Eden Lodge in the early years of the 17th century. (Bride, Old Leigh, p. 40.) For a period it was a licensed house under different names (The Queen's Head, The Angel, and The King's Head). For a short time in the last century it was part of a distillery producing gin, but later it reverted to a private residence again. After it ceased to be licensed premises or part of a distillery it was occupied by a Mr. Henry Thompson who was the church organist in Victorian times. He is said to have been the protege of Rev. Robert Eden, who recognised musical ability in him. In this house lived also Mrs. Thackeray (wife of William Makepeace Thackeray, the author) after their separation. The lady is buried in Leigh cemetery. The older people still remember Eden Lodge which was demolished about the turn of the century.

35. View up Leigh Hill in the 1890s. On the right is Fred Joscelyn's blacksmith's shop. The family had been in Leigh, and mostly in this part of the parish, since the 18th century. Farther on Mrs. F. Brewer is standing at the door of her butcher's shop. Speaking of poverty and distress in Victorian Leigh, H. N. Bride writes 'Occasionally distress was so acute that a soup kitchen was opened in 1886. It was at Mrs. F. Brewer's; the days were Tuesdays, Thursdays and Saturdays and the soup was sold at 1½d. a quart'. (Bride, Old Leigh, p. 56.) The Southend Standard of 16 April 1886 wrote 'The soup Kitchen at Mrs. F. Brewer's which during the winter has proved a boon to many poor families in Leigh, through the low price at which good soup was supplied, closed its winter's work on Saturday last'.

36. Church Hill from the Leigh Hill end. Although the hill has the ancient charm of a Devon village scene, only the buildings on the near right are older than the 19th century. Near here was the free school which Sir Samuel Moyer—one of the mariner family of that name —founded in 1716 'for instructing children in the principles of the Christian religion'. (Benton, p. 339) There were no Charity Commissioners in those days to keep an eye on such schools, and at some point in the 18th century it disappeared, and the buildings were sold. Robert Eden, the Rector, founded in 1847 the National School at the top of the hill on the right. The white stone pillars are the extremities of the school boundary wall. Everything on the right of the picture has been re-developed.

37. Shops on the south side of Leigh Hill. The picture dates back to the early years of the present century.

38. Leigh Hill, looking downhill. The old cottages have now gone. The kindly old gentleman in the road is thought to be one of the Emery family who lived near here.

39. Old Cottages south of Leigh Hill. They were situated well back on the south side of the hill. The sea and a small boat can be seen on the extreme left, thus helping us to identify the site of the cottages. They were demolished at the latter part of the 19th century.

40. The same cottages south of Leigh Hill. This is the view of the cottages from the other side. Note the tower of St. Clement's at the extreme right in the distance.

THE BANK HOUSE AND ITS GLASS

On the south side of Leigh Hill, farther up than the shops is a house abutting the pavement, but with a long garden overlooking the sea. It was probably built early in the last century or perhaps a little before. It could not be called a house of distinction except for its situation but a window on the south side contains four roundels of glass which are interesting and which give rise to certain problems adding to their interest. The origin of the roundels is unknown and there is reason for thinking they are not all of the same date. (The author is greatly indebted to Dr. W. J. Petchey, headmaster of Ripon Grammar School and to Mr. A. C. Edwards.)

41. The man seated and holding a sceptre. This is the Black Prince, and here his seal is reproduced. The Latin surround can be translated 'Seal of Edward, eldest son of the King of England, Prince of Aquitaine and Wales, Duke of Cornwall and Earl of Chester'. It is probably work of the mid-19th century (Gothic Revival, as it is generally called).

42. (*above left*) The Crowned Lady with the kneeling man. The wheel shows that this is St. Catherine, but the man is unidentified. The saint is in antique clothing, and the style together with the brocaded panel, suggests a late Flemish 17th century painting, although the man's costume is of 1500-1550 date. Either the glass is continental of 17th century or a 19th century imitation.

43. (*above right*) Coat of Arms. This is the coat of arms of a man, but it is definitely continental—German or Swiss of possibly the early 17th century. We have been unable to discover whose arms they were.

44. (*left*) Coat of Arms. This is the armorial bearings of a lady. The date is the same as 43, and also similar in other respects. There is little doubt that these four pieces of glass were acquired second hand from an antique dealer and inserted during the last century. Pieces of glass of this sort were frequently sold at that time. There is no need to assume that the four pieces had a common origin.

Leigh Essex

No. 1014

...haw & Son, London

45.   Etching of Leigh Hill. As the bell turret of the National School is depicted near the top right the date must be after 1847. There is no development on the north side below the row at the top which still exists. On the south side there is nothing on this side of the Bank House. Note the chimney at the bottom left hand corner. The map of 1845 marks at this spot 'Old lime kiln'.

46. Rev. Edmund Worlledge's sketch of Leigh Hill in 1844. This is probably fairly accurate in detail, and is rather earlier than the previous illustration. The Bank House is there, but the National School had not been built, nor is there any building above the cottages on the north side with dormer windows. This coincides with contemporary maps. Down the hill the road seems partly obstructed by a gate. Was there in fact a toll gate at this point, giving to the road the name, previously mentioned, Turnpike Hill? The author does not know the answer to the question.

47. View from Rev. Edmund Worlledge's House. The title on the sketch is 'South view towards Southend from my window'. It could have been that he lived in one of the cottages at the right of the last picture. Alternatively he could have lived at Prospect House, higher up the hill. Either would give such a view as this. Note the short Southend Pier in the far distance and the craft, including a schooner in the estuary.

VII THE LEIGH FORESHORE

The sea has remained unchanged for centuries, but the foreshore and the view of Leigh from the sea have changed continuously since man first settled here. It is impossible to imagine what the foreshore was like in the days when the Haddocks, the Goodlads, the Salmons and the members of other mariner families sailed their craft into Leigh Creek. Bell Wharf was not built until the early years of the last century. When were the other wharves made? Where did the old ships berth? What did the foreshore look like when they were in their home port? Admiral Blake brought his damaged fleet into Leigh for repair in 1652. Where was the work done? Where were the ships built, for records show that Leigh was a shipbuilding port in Tudor times? These are all questions we should like to be able to answer, but, alas, no pictures or drawings or written records have come down to us.

There has long been an unsolved problem: to what extent has Leigh Creek and the channels that it enters changed during the course of the last few centuries? Did the draining of the marshes west and south west of Leigh cause a silting up of the channels leading into Leigh? What was the effect of Southend Pier on the Swatchway by which ships used to enter Leigh. There is a well known passage in John Wesley's Diaries for 1748, oft quoted, 'Here was once a deep open harbour, but the sands have long since blocked it up'.

The first illustrations of the foreshore that have come down to us were in the form of prints made from etchings produced in the first half of the last century. They were largely used to illustrate topographical books.

Some artists came and made pictures in oil or water colour. What a pity John Constable, who is reputed to have stayed at the dwelling we knew as Juniper's shop when he came to paint Hadleigh Castle, did not stay longer and paint one of Leigh foreshore.

One has to question how much the artists have given us in their pictures is real and exact, and how much is 'artists' licence'. None the less the artists do convey an impression of what the place was like as they saw it and of the general atmosphere that prevailed.

The coming of photography brought in realism, showing us buildings and objects as they really were in their relative positions. Photography came too late to provide us with all the information we should have liked, but we must be profoundly thankful that it arrived in time to record so much that has been destroyed in the last century.

The collection of pictures shown here draws on prints, paintings and photographs. All who are interested will find a splendid collection of Leigh pictures in the Beecroft Art Gallery, especially of works whose interest is in their artistic merit rather than a realistic representation of what old Leigh was really like.

THE VILLAGE OF LEIGH, NEAR SOUTHEND.
ESSEX.

Drawn by W. Bartlett. Engraved by C. Mottram

48.   A print 'The Village of Leigh near Southend'. This was drawn by William Henry Bartlett the first (1809-54) and engraved by Charles Mottram (1807-76). It was published in 1833. It is not possible to identify the wharves and buildings though some of the buildings on the extreme left correspond both to a map and to Fripp's picture of 1852. The old Rectory pulled down in 1838 is visible at the top left corner. The poplar trees which were on the Rectory lawn until recent times are also to be seen. The building with a tower in the middle of the picture is somewhat a mystery, though an old map places 'the old lime kiln' on a site in that direction. The real problem is to identify the type of fishing boats so prominent in the picture. Mr. Hervey Benham, an authority on Essex fishing craft, writes 'The portrayal of the fishing craft is unconvincing. Probably they are intended to represent the little London river peter boats which preceded the bawleys. Of the pair in the foreground that on the left has a net pulled up to the mast head to dry, while that on the right has apparently an ill drawn lugsail with loops on the luff which are probably mast hoops, but the artist does not understand that they should encircle the mast. Behind them is a roughly stowed spritsail with square topsail, but it is difficult to see which boat it belongs to.' We ought perhaps to write off some of these anomalies as 'artist's licence'.

49. Leigh from the marshes. Here we have a clear picture of the old town about 1870-1880 before the wholesale destruction of the old houses had begun. Though there is some development in the east, Leigh Park Road and Hadleigh Road had not yet been begun. Bawleys, cockle boats and barges are moored along different parts of the foreshore.

50. Low Tide at Leigh. This is from a water colour drawing by Adam Forsyth, R.A. He exhibited in 1889-92, and showed two pictures at the New Water Colour society in 1889-91. This picture is certainly before those dates. The tall building with chimney and what appears to be a black tank for tar or a condenser may be the newly founded Gas Works. Sheds on the Victoria Wharf can be identified. Like many pictures of Leigh from the sea side, the slopes are shown well wooded. The picture is a work of art rather than a realistic representation.

51. Leigh Old Town from the Marshes. This is another picture of the Old Town before the demolition began. In the centre can be seen the houses to the east of the Strand with their dormer windows. The Bell Wharf is just included on the right side, but the picture does not go as far west as the Billet Wharf. The fisherman is the late Mr. Bill Little who had two fish pits on this piece of marsh where he stored fish alive when he caught more than he could handle or wanted to send to market. There were seven fish ponds here earlier in the last century. (Benton, pp. 377-8.)

52. Leigh from the Marshes, a later picture. The picture was taken before the turn of the century. Leigh Park Road and Hadleigh Road have just begun to be built. The New Road Methodist Church is just included at the extreme left, but the picture does not go as far east as the Strand. At the top right you can see the poplar trees in the old Rectory garden. Pittington House is right in the middle of the picture.

BILLET QUAY, LEIGH-ON-SEA.

53. Foreshore from the Billet Wharf, looking eastwards. This is a 19th-century etching, and the details are accurate. The object lying on the shore is a discarded windlass from a bawley. The bawleys had a windlass near the bow operated by hand levers. On the later (and larger) bawleys they had a winch with a handle to haul up the net. The vessel in the picture is an early clinker-built bawley.

54. From the Bell Wharf in the 1890s. There was no 'cinder path' to Westcliff nor any beaches artificially made. The coal and goods yard was behind the white fence by the side of the railway. The black building on the shore was Bundock's boat building shed. Thomas Bundock started boatbuilding in Leigh about 1813, and the trade was carried on by his son and grandsons until 1943. (Bride, Old Leigh, pp. 39-40.) The white building adjoining was the Coastguard station. In the distance can be seen 'The Gypsy', the first headquarters of the Essex Yacht Club.

55. Old steps from the quay to the water. These are at the back of Richard Chester's house on the Strand and may well date back to his time.

56. Coastguard Station, looking east towards Bell Wharf. Smuggling was a feature of the life of Leigh in the 18th and 19th centuries. Many stories used to be told of Leigh fishermen smuggling spirits and tobacco ashore to sell, and so to augment their meagre living. The job of the coastguards was to combat the traffic. In 1851 there were six coastguards, and Thomas Garland was their Chief Officer. (Bride, Old Leigh, p. 40.) They wore uniforms similar to seamen in the Royal Navy. It is noteworthy that in the list of coastguards in the 1851 census they were all born in distant parts of the country. No doubt to avoid collusion with the natives the authorities sent men from afar with no local contacts. The Coastguard station continued in this site until about the turn of the century. The railway then enlarged the 'up' platform and the goods sidings, and the 'cinder path' to Westcliff was made.

57. View of the 'up' platform and goods siding. This was taken from the Bell footbridge which no longer exists. It was like this until the new station in Belton Way came in 1933.

VIII THE CHURCH

The crowning glory of Old Leigh is St. Clement's Church standing on its incomparable position with its massive tall tower overlooking the estuary, a beacon for those at sea and a sentinel over the village community.

It is strange that while so much of the cliff, both east and west of the church, has experienced serious subsidence, the ground around the church shows little sign of movement.

Some may ask why this particular spot was chosen for the parish church. While the people lived down the hill their church was at the top of it. The answer may be that the lord of the manor chose a site near his own house (Leigh Hall) and in the direction where the villagers lived. This spot too was at the meeting of the only roads in Leigh. Also an explanation may be found in the partiality of pre-Norman church builders to choose sites on the summits of hills. This is very true for south Essex. There is no doubt, too, that many churches were built on the site of pagan (pre-Christian) sanctuaries. There is no evidence of there ever being an ancient church in any other part of Leigh.

Not a great deal is known about the early history of St. Clement's. There was nothing unusual about it during the Middle Ages, and it passed through the Reformation period like other English churches. In common with most Essex churches it was extremely Puritan. It was in the 19th century and subsequently that great changes in the building and its setting were made. Until then it was a country church in a purely rural setting. By the end of the 19th century it was a town church serving an increasingly urban community.

However, this was not the only change that St. Clement's experienced. By the 19th century many churches had gone several centuries without restoration or attention to the structure, so most old churches went through a 19th century restoration. Unfortunately the earlier restorers had not yet learnt to value and appreciate much that had survived from a former age, and features which nowadays would be preserved and venerated were swept away wholesale. Robert Eden (Rector 1837-51) embarked on one of these earlier restorations. Some writers have been critical of Eden. That St. Clement's was heavily restored at this time is certain, but how much disappeared which now would be valued is largely conjectural. No detailed plans or a description of the Eden restoration appear to exist.

There are some unsolved problems in the structure and contents of St. Clement's. When were the embattlements removed from the red brick Tudor porch? What is the date of the poppy-headed pews in the nave and north aisle, and when were they introduced into the church? What is the origin of the east window of the crucifixion? The same question arises over the two-light window in the south wall of the sanctuary, though in this case we know that this design for painted glass was by Sir Joshua Reynolds and exhibited at the Royal Academy in 1779.

As the arms of Lady Sparrow and Dr. Eden are incorporated into this window there is a strong presupposition that they gave it, and that it went into the church at the Eden restoration.

In 1872, to meet the needs of the times, the chancel was extended eastwards. This was the first change in the ground plan for at least 400 years. In 1897 the south aisle was added and the medieval south wall pierced with an arcade. Not until 1913 was the effort completed by the building of the Lady Chapel. At the same time the vestries at the north east corner of the church were built—a project which mutilated some of the medieval east window in the north aisle.

Fortunately an adequate supply of pictures of the exterior of the church has come down to us to see what the building looked like as it was from the Middle Ages onwards and at every stage during the 19th century changes, but owing to the absence of prints after 1840 and of good photographs, our supply of interiors is poor.

It is not the aim of this book to include photographs of buildings, objects or people that can be seen in Leigh at the present day. For that reason objects of interest in the church and churchyard are not to be found in this section. The reader can go and see the real thing for himself. An exception has been made in some of the monumental brasses which appear in another section and are in another context (See plate 111), and in any case cannot readily be found in the church by the ordinary visitor.

58.   St. Clement's Church exterior in 1786. The author believes this to be the oldest illustration of St. Clement's in existence. It is a colour drawing in a collection belonging to Chelmsford District Public Library, and we publish it by kind permission of Mr. S. M. Jarvis, F.L.A., District Librarian. The same applies to the next picture which is also in the Chelmsford District Library. The artist is unknown. We notice how wonderfully rural the setting was in 1786. It is difficult to place the dwelling house on the extreme left. It is where one would expect to see Leigh House, but it is the wrong shape. It might be the cottage marked on the map north of the church, moved a little, out of 'artist's licence'. The lane to the west end of the churchyard corresponds with the road on the map, described in the section on Leigh Hill. Obviously there is no Church Hill in the picture, and the road serves as the way to the old town as well as being the drive to the Rectory which at this date was very near to Chess Lane (see map). The church tower is much the same as now, except for the turret—and for this there is an explanation later. As for the rest of the building: there is no south aisle, the porch is embattled and the porch window appears unglazed. The picture is St. Clement's as it was throughout the ages in a quiet rural setting. Certainly it had remained unchanged from the early Tudor times when the red brick porch was put on, and probably that porch merely replaced one on the same site in medieval style.

59. St. Clement's Church in 1787. This is less a work of art than an architect's drawing. It is enscribed 'J. T. Smith delin.' and is dated. It is now in Chelmsford District Library. The picture confirms that the porch was once embattled, but the sundial (shown in the last picture) is omitted. The chancel and north chapel are lower than the nave. There is a priest's doorway and two small windows in the chancel south wall. The nave south windows look as if the artist has simplified them by omitting tracery that ought to be there. He has certainly done the same with the two east windows, thus taking away from us valuable information we should like to know. The tree (or is it ivy?) persists on the south wall of the tower.

60. The Church after about 1800. This is a well known print published by Sarjint of 57 John Street, Fitzroy Square, London. Some editions of it are tinted. In many respects it resembles the picture of the church in 1786. We still have the entirely rural setting and no house in sight. Note that once again the porch is embattled and this time the sundial is shown. We also have further evidence of Chess Lane and the absence of Church Hill at this time.

61. The Church from the east in 1836. This delightful pencil drawing is in the Thorpe Smith collection in the Beecroft Art Gallery, Southend (No. 39) and it is unascribed. The view is from what is now the Broadway, but then called Hall Road. The chancel roof is lower than the nave roof. This is what we should expect before the Eden restoration. A chimney pipe seems to come out of the east window of the north aisle. The buildings on the left are Prospect House and Herschell House, now called Ivy Cottage. There is a single cottage on the north side which may be one owned by Captain Richard Tanner in the Tithe Award of 1847.

62. The south side of the Church in 1844 by Edmund Worlledge. Here we have the building after Dr. Eden's restoration. There is every reason for thinking that Worlledge was accurate in his detail. No south aisle had yet been added, but the embattlements have gone from the porch and they are replaced by the gable that still exists. The east window is of the decorated period (1300 A.D.) and may well have been the original medieval window. The chancel door shown here went in the 1913 extension. The chancel roof is now as high as the nave roof. There is only a fence round the church-yard; the substantial stone wall had not yet been built. However, the high brick wall along the east boundary of Leigh House had now been built, and it was not destroyed until the row of shops was built in the 1920s. A chimney of the new Rectory can be seen amongst the trees. The gravedigger wears a top hat—the fashion for all in those days.

63. The east end before 1872. In 1872 the chancel (the left hand gable in the picture) was extended outwards. This shows what it was like before the extension. The window of the decorated period (about 1300 A.D.) can be clearly seen. It was rebuilt in the same style, perhaps with the same stone tracery, in the 1872 extension. Compare the decorated window with the perpendicular window on the right, the style of which is a century later. Except for the damage to it when the new vestry was built it remains the same as when it was put there in the 1400s.

64. The east end after 1872. A Leigh amateur artist, Miss A. M. Marsh, painted this picture of the east end from the field opposite the church before the houses were built (Carlton Terrace). Carlton Terrace was built in 1886 so it would seem that the picture must be before that date. It can be dated after 1872 because the chancel had been extended, but before 1889 when the clock was introduced into the tower.

65. Disaster to the Tower. On Sunday 25 October 1896, during a violent thunder storm, the church was struck by lightning. The flash struck the turret of the tower, and according to contemporary accounts went out at the top of the east window of the chancel. Our picture shows the turret with much of the stone work and masonry displaced. When it was repaired a certain amount of rebuilding of the turret was necessary because cracking caused instability. The Southend Standard of 30 October 1896 printed this account of the incident: 'The morning service had concluded about ten minutes when the storm reached its height, it being accompanied by a heavy downpour of hailstones. The housekeeper at Leigh House was watching the storm over the water, and suddenly she saw something apparently of the shape of a ball of bluish fire descend and strike the road on the north side of the church. At the same time Coastguard Fiddes, who lives opposite the church, saw smoke from the tower, and surmising that it had been struck by the electric fluid, he ran at once to the Rectory. The Rector, Rev. R.S. King, who was in his study watching the storm, having just left the church after service, at once returned and saw on his arrival that a number of parishioners had assembled. Messrs. E. Thompson and S. Hipsey, having burst open the steeple door and Coastguard Fiddes with Messrs. E. and W. Thorp, bellringers, knowing

the position of the bells, made their way to the seat of the fire and by means of pails of water all danger of conflagration was immediately ended. It was then learnt that the tower had been struck on the north side causing fire to the belfry. The danger was great on account of some disused sawdust, packed round a window some years ago to deaden the sound of the bells because of a person lying ill in the neighbourhood, not having been removed. The current was traced from the belfry down into the ropery into some beading on the side of the wall, where it was lost. The bells were uninjured. In the evening the Rector conducted a Thanksgiving Service, preaching a suitable sermon to a large congregation. After the ordinary service Jackson's 'Te Deum' was sung by the congregation and choir.

66. An early interior of St. Clement's. This is a copy of a print, the original being 18 inches by 11½ inches. The drawing was on stone by W. L. Walton, and the printer was C. J. Hullmandell. The former was working between 1834 and 1855, but the latter died in 1850. Thus it could be dated between 1834 and 1850. It was probably made after the restoration by Dr. Eden, say about 1840. Some present features are easily recognisable in the picture, such as the north arcade and the chancel arch. There is no south arcade as the south aisle was not built until 1897. Here we see the medieval south wall and windows. The chancel had not yet been lengthened as this was not done until 1872, but the east window of the Crucifixion appears much as it is today, except that the tracery is different and belongs to the decorated period (1300). The altar is as one would expect at that time, small and simple, covered with a frontal ornamented with the IHS monogram. At each end are cushions for books whilst the almsdish, again ornamented with IHS, is in the centre. The pulpit stands on the south side and is higher than one would expect. It would seem to be the same pulpit that was displaced 20 years ago, having been both reduced in height and transferred to the other side in the intervening period. The poppy-headed pews which cover most of the nave and north aisle are of uncertain age. No one seems to know if they were first introduced into St. Clement's at the Eden restoration, and, if this were the case, were they new when they were introduced? There are questions about them that we cannot answer. In the picture many of them face south. Some of them were re-orientated at the 1872 restoration, but the rest were not turned to the east until 1913. The Lord's Prayer, the Apostles' Creed and the Decalogue adorn the east wall. Benton says the canopies over them were of stucco. The people in their contemporary costume add some life and interest to the picture. We hope the good folk of Leigh were as devout and prayerful in that period as the picture suggests. Finally we observe there were no choir stalls; the singing at that time was led by an orchestra in a west gallery. The Rector had his stall by the pulpit. However, about this time Dr. Eden introduced the first organ into St. Clement's.

67. Mural painting in St. Clement's. One of the features that accompanied the revival in interest in Church architecture in the last century was the re-introduction of mural paintings—scriptural scenes or saints painted on the wall. A local craftsman, George Brewer, painted the four evangelists on the east wall and the Baptism of Christ on the wall behind the font. Then came the time when everything Victorian was deemed bad artistically and much was destroyed in consequence. Not until the time of Sir John Betjeman was this view of Victorian art modified, but the change came too late. In the early fifties Brewer's work was lime washed (or covered with emulsion paint) so it is no longer visible. Our picture shows the Baptism of our Lord before it was covered over. The author has not been able to find any very clear pictures of Brewer's four Evangelists.

BY ONE SPIRIT ARE WE ALL BAPTIZED INTO ONE BODY

IX THE RECTORY—NOW THE PUBLIC LIBRARY

We have some knowledge of four different buildings used as the Rectory in Leigh. One was built (or perhaps rebuilt on the same site) by Rev. J. D. Hodge after he was instituted in 1793. It was south of the present Library and nearer the cliff edge. Benton describes it as 'of white brick, weather boarded at the back and ends. The roof was a single one tiled, and with gable ends'. No trace of this remains.[1]

Robert Eden who came as Rector in 1837 was a rich man from a titled family and he wanted a more pretentious home. So he had the old Rectory pulled down and a much larger new one built. This new Rectory became the present Leigh Public Library with certain notable changes. As a Rectory it was built round four sides of a square, the kitchen and domestic outhouses occupying three sides of the square. These were removed when the Southend Corporation acquired the building leaving only the front which was the largest and most elegant part. The porch which was formerly on the east side was rebuilt brick by brick in its present position on the north side. Broadway West passes over the site of the old domestic buildings and the Rectory yard. The interior of the Rectory was changed out of all recognition when it was converted into the Library. The ecclesiastical origin of the building is shown by the arms of the see of London over the porch—Leigh being in the diocese of London at that time.

Besides a large garden round three sides of the house there was a glebe field which extended to the western end of Rectory Grove, and a kitchen garden which extended nearly to the eastern end of Rectory Grove opposite the present Post Office. All this has largely been built over.

The new Rectory, used from 1925, is the building now called Watson House. Later, the Old School south of the church became the Rector's house, and it still remains so.

The Eden Rectory was too large by far for the dwelling of a humble parish priest, and the gardens and grounds far too big for anyone but a business tycoon to keep up. None the less there was an exquisite beauty and charm about the house and its grounds that none who can remember them in the old days will ever forget. We must be grateful that most of the house remains—as the Library, and part of the gardens—especially that overlooking the estuary, has survived for posterity.

Note
1. Benton p. 376.

68. The Rectory from the south east by Edmund Worlledge. The building was scarcely seven years old when Edmund Worlledge portrayed it as a pencil drawing in 1844. Note the porch on the east side, whereas it is now on the north. Apart from the layout of the gardens and growth of trees this picture is the same as many will remember in their youth.

69. The Rectory, view from the north west about 1895. The front of the building appears virtually the same as it is today. the corner room was the drawing room, the middle room with the bay window was the Rector's study, whilst at the further end was the dining room. The seated figure in the garden is Canon Robert King. There is a holly bush on the right into which new choir boys used to be thrown on their first appearance as an 'initiation ceremony'. The author went through this experience on a dark and wet night.

70. The Rectory, north west corner. This is the west side of the old Rectory Garden, together with the conservatory. The trees on the left and the conservatory have gone and their site is covered by the present road. The glebe meadow, now occupied by the blocks of flats and St. Clement's Hall, was on this side of the Rectory.

71. Although in the first instance the main drive into the Rectory was from the Church end, ultimately the principal approach was made from Rectory Grove. The main gates were at the top of Lymington Avenue, and there was a most picturesque drive up to the house with tall trees on either side, and a profusion of bulbs flowering during the spring in the beds beneath. Scores of rooks nested in the trees overhead with consequences during the season that require little imagination. The picture we show is a snow scene. Note the porch in its former position on the east of the building. Most of the picture is at present occupied by offices and shops.

X LEIGH HOUSE

This residence, originally known as Black House, stood near the church to the north west (No. 3 on the map). The pedestrian crossing and the first shops in Elm Road (west side) occupy the site. Its garden extended north, west and south. That to the west bounded the Rectory garden, while part of that to the south still exists and extends to the path along the cliff edge.

The house is thought to have been built about 1620. Stephen Bonner owned it and probably lived in it at the time when he made his will in 1644. Sir Anthony Deane, naval architect and friend of Samuel Pepys, later owned it and used it as an occasional residence until 1670 when he sold it to Thomas Printupp. There are Printupps buried in the church.

Other owners were Elizabeth Stevens, Anne, wife of Sir Edward Whittaker (who was Admiral of the White), Charles Perry, Elizabeth and John Finch, and Giles Westwood.[1] The next holder was John Loten (1792 until 1815), Collector of Customs at Leigh. He planted two cedar trees in the garden which have survived to this day. He also planted ivy both on the walls of Leigh House and on the church tower. In both cases the ivy was removed in this century as detrimental to the structures.

David Montague, then P.C. Barker followed at Leigh House. F. J. C. Millar was the owner in late Victorian times. He was the donor of the clock in the church tower. The last owner was Dr. W. D. Watson.

As with many old houses it had at one time its tale that it was haunted. Added to this is the story that in Loten's time a female human skeleton was dug up from under the floor.

Note
1. Benton, p. 333.

72.   Leigh House, east front. This is the view one would get approaching the house from the Broadway. It was demolished to make room for Broadway West. Part of the ivy (which used to cover all the front wall) can still be seen at the side. The cedar trees which still exist are to the left of the picture.

73.   Leigh House, west front. Broadway West now passes over the site of the house. Some boughs of one of the cedar trees can be seen on the right.

74. In Leigh House garden under one of the cedar trees. Some of the trees at the back of the photograph were in the Rectory garden. This picture was taken from the church tower.

75. From the garden of Leigh House in 1844. It is hard to believe this picture; time has so altered the appearance of everything—no Church Hill, no Old Schools (which are now the Rectory), no churchyard wall. The church itself is out of sight to the left. The large houses which dominate the left of the picture are Herschell House and Prospect House. The owner and occupant of Leigh House in 1844 was Mr. David Montague who owned Leigh Pottery and Brickworks.

XI LEIGH HALL

Leigh Hall was the Mansion House or Manor House of the Manor of Leigh. As the Domesday Survey of 1085 tells us, the manor[1] was held, with other local manors by Ranulf. Then for nearly 250 years we know nothing of its owners until 'John de Arpeton' as Lord of Legra (Leigh) appointed a Rector. From 1337 until 1673 the manor of Leigh was held by the owners of the manor of Rochford, and they included, at different times, the families of Rochford, Bohun, Boteler, Bullen or Boleyn, Riche and the Earl of Warwick. Benton and others give a complete list, and as the ownership passed through daughters into other families the study becomes extremely complicated. In the 19th century the manor came into the possession of Brigadier Sir Robert Bernard Sparrow of Worlingham in Suffolk, who married Lady Olivia Acheson, eldest daughter of the Earl of Gosforth. On his early death, his widow, Lady Olivia Bernard Sparrow, became Lady of the Manor of Leigh. Lady Olivia died in 1863. Her child, a daughter who had married the Duke of Manchester, had died in 1848, so their two sons were Lady Olivia's heirs. They sold the manor and Leigh property. The manor house, Leigh Hall, was bought by a Deptford coal merchant, Thomas Smith, and the manor rights by one, Ernest Wild. Later in the last century the Churchyard family acquired the manor rights, which were sold by Mrs. Mary Churchyard to Mr. William Theobald, the wharf and barge owner, early this century. At his death the manorial rights were acquired by Southend Corporation. No doubt as the manor owned the Strand and enjoyed certain rights on the foreshore the Corporation thought it prudent that these should no longer remain in possession of a private individual

The manorial house, known as Leigh Hall, was situated south of the present Pall Mall, and between Leigh Hall Road and Oakleigh Park Drive. From the Hall there was a wonderful view of the estuary unimpeded by any buildings as the fields and cliffs sloped away to the sea. Except for the pottery on the one side (to the east) and the church and half a dozen houses (to the west) the view until the last two decades of the 19th century was entirely rural.

Leigh Hall itself, from existing pictures, appears to have been Elizabethan. Benton gives the date as 1561,[2] but he also says that it had a west wing, the foundations of which remained. No doubt there was much earlier work and many features which have never been recorded.

The house and all the farm land belonging to it were sold late in the last century, and sporadic house building over the land began. The Broadway at first was a road for dwelling houses. Then later, shops appeared, or the houses were converted into shops. The Hall itself survived until just after 1900. The Bentall family were the last tenants and farmed the land until they were compelled to surrender to the speculative builder.

Notes
1. Benton, pp. 317-8.
2. Benton, p. 316

76. Leigh Hall from the south, (I). This is the side of the house you would have seen from the site of the present Broadway, originally a narrow country road called Hall Road. There was a field between the road and the house where cricket was played and village functions were held. The hall was a typically Essex farmhouse with upper storey slightly overhanging the lower, and if Benton's surmise is correct there was a wing at the west (left) and at right angles to the portrayed building. The chimney stacks, no doubt in red brick, were typical.

77. Leigh Hall, the House (II). This is from the same side and the picture gives a better idea of the intensely rural nature of the setting. There are the cows grazing in the meadow, and the little coppice of trees beyond. At the time of writing there are still Leigh folk who can remember Leigh Hall as it is seen here. Mrs. Frances Boulton of Rochford, whose father was Mr. Bentall, lived here in her infancy and still remembers it like this.

78.   Leigh Hall from the north west. Here we have the other side of the house, giving us evidence of the period when it was built. If Benton was right the old wing that he thought once existed ran across the right end of the house.

79.   Leigh Hall, the pond. The pond was to the extreme west of the farm and farm buildings, and it was much larger than it appears from the small part visible in the picture. The horse-drawn vehicle appears to be a water cart and it is moving down the chase from the Hall to the Hall Road.

80. Leigh Hall from the south west. The corner of the house is on the right, and here we see some of the fine trees to the west of it and some of the farm buildings.

81. Leigh Hall, the farmyard. Here we see some of the buildings to the west and north-west of the Hall. Such a fine tree as we see here would nowadays be scheduled for preservation.

XII THE OLD SCHOOLS—NOW THE RECTORY

No state education was provided in England until the 1870 Education Act became law, though from the early part of that century the state gave a certain amount of financial help, not on a very generous scale, to those who were running voluntary schools. These were, for the most part, schools that had been founded by Christian people and endowed, with a strongly religious motive behind them. As we have already seen, Sir Samuel Moyer founded 'a free school' early in the 18th century sited north of Leigh Hill somewhere near to what is now the foot of Church Hill, but this did not survive.[1]

Lady Olivia Sparrow, to whom we devote attention later on, founded a school which was sited on the north side of what is now the Broadway, and roughly behind the present Woolworths (No. 4 on the map). It appears that the school was not secured by a legal trust and when she died in 1863 the school was sold up with the rest of her estate.

However, the Church of England was the greatest sponsor of popular education and most of its schools were founded under the auspices of the National Society. At the same time the Nonconformists, who also were patrons of popular education, founded theirs under the auspices of the British Schools Society.

Lady Sparrow, though an Anglican, was of the opposite school of thought to the Rector, Robert Eden, who was a great supporter of the National Society. He and the good lady clashed over school policy in Leigh and probably because the legal foundation of her school was rather nebulous, himself in 1847 founded a National School, giving the land and paying for the cost of the building himself.

It was on the site—before then unoccupied—immediately to the south of the church, on the hill. The building in Kentish ragstone was the shape of an E without the middle horizontal arm.

Being built on a slope with foundations inadequate in the Leigh clay, and in heavy stone, there was considerable settlement, and the structure gave a lot of trouble. To make adequate repairs as well as to pay the staff was beyond the capacity of the Church. Thus, ultimately, when the 1870 Act began to operate, thoughts were turned to building a state school under the control of a School Board.

This materialised with the founding of North Street School and the closure of the Church School. The south wing of the old school and part of the middle section were demolished as unsafe. The upper wing was used for Church purposes as a hall, and in 1926 it was sold to Mr. W. G. Beecroft who tastefully converted it into a dwelling house. Then in the 1950s it was bought back by the Church as the Rectory.

Note
1. Benton, p. 339.

82. The Old Church School. The upper wing (left of the picture) was the Girls' School. The lower wing was the Boys' School. The picture was taken about the beginning of the present century when the Boys' School was derelict and the upper building was little used. The boundary wall and stone pillars are still there, as also are the upper building and the terrace around it.

83. The Old Schools, looking up the hill. The main building is the Girls' School. Beyond it in the corner is the residence of the Headmaster and his wife. Henry Simpson was headmaster in 1851 and his daughter, Susan, a schoolmistress. Mr. and Mrs. Ray were there at a later period until 1889 when Mr. A. H. Thatcher was appointed. The latter was shortly afterwards appointed head of the newly founded Board School and remained until 1926.

84. (*above*) Demolition of the Boys'
School in 1913. Fred Phillips, the verger
of St. Clement's, is in the middle of the
picture wielding the pick axe.

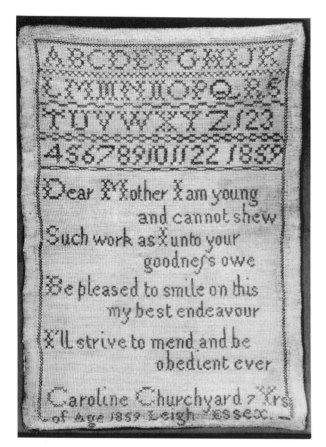

ABCDEFGHIJK
LMMNNOPQRS
TUVWXYZ123
456789101122 1859

Dear Mother I am young
and cannot shew
Such work as I unto your
goodnefs owe
Be pleased to smile on this
my best endeavour
I'll strive to mend and be
obedient ever

Caroline Churchyard 7 Yrs
of Age 1859 Leigh Essex

85. (*left*) A Leigh child's work. We
include this picture of a sampler made by
a Leigh girl, Caroline Churchyard, in
1859. It is 9 inches by 6¼ inches. We are
not entirely certain that she did go to the
school. Her father, George Churchyard,
was a blacksmith and ships chandler in
Leigh.

XIII THE HINTERLAND OF LEIGH

This expression is meant to include all that part of Leigh above the cliffs and out to the parish boundaries. Until the middle of the last century the whole of this area was agricultural or woodland with but a few isolated dwellings. The boundary points of Leigh were the Burnt Post (towards Hadleigh), the dip in the London Road where Cricketfield Grove is now, the site of the present Belfairs Club House and the site of the Fire Station in Blenheim Chase.

We have already mentioned the Rectory, Leigh House and Leigh Hall. A little farther east were Oak Farm and the Pottery. There was nothing more until you reached the London Road, and in 1845 there were only four dwellings on it, Leigh Heath Farm, Leigh Park Farm, Lapwater Hall and the Elm. Then right away to the north were Belfairs Farm House, Gowles Farm and Brickhouse Farm.

Our pictures in this section will show what it was like before development took place and during the early days of growth.

86. First shop in the Broadway. This was on the corner of West Street. It was a grocer's shop, and Mr. James Nash was the first proprietor. The date was in the late 1880s. Mr. Harry Payne followed Mr. Nash as proprietor.

87. The Church and Broadway about 1890. The Broadway—formerly called Hall Road or Leigh Hall Road—began to be built up purely as a residential road. To this day you can see the old houses (1880 style) with shop-fronts superimposed on them. The trees (including the cedars) of Leigh House garden are in the centre of the picture. There was no Broadway West in those days.

88. The top of Leigh Hill. No shops opposite the church yet—Leigh House was still there clad in ivy. However, the trams have arrived providing a service to Southend High Street. The fares until after the World War I were two old pence (less than 1p in present coinage) for an adult to Southend and one old penny for children. Note the open top trams. You were supplied with waterproof aprons on wet days. Date: about the turn of the century, perhaps just before 1900.

89. Church corner in 1910 or earlier. This was the terminus of the trams to Southend. They derived their electricity from overhead wires via the arm which had to be turned round at the end of each journey and often came off in between. The cab rank by the church wall was principally for cabs to Hadleigh, there being no buses going there in those days. The cost was 4d. per person. Hence they were commonly called the 'Hadleigh fourpennies'. The only road to Hadleigh was via Elm Road, past the Elm Hotel and thence up the London Road.

90. Elm Road in about 1870. The view is from the east side of Elm Road close to the present Methodist Church. From this stile there proceeded two footpaths, one (on the right) leading to Leigh Hall, the farm buildings of which are in the distance. The other footpath led to the left and it was a short cut to the Elm Farm (not a public house in those days).

91. Elm Road from the Rectory Grove Corner about 1890. As with the Broadway so also with Elm Road: it began as a residential road when development first took place. Most of the right side was taken up by Leigh House and its garden except at the near end where there was a large corner house which had been built for Mr. John Osborne. His house can still be seen behind shop fronts.

92. Elm Road about 1920. Leigh House stands on the right, but a cinema (The Coliseum) is just out of sight on the right. It is now the bingo hall. On the left beyond the two houses is a building first called the Sailors' Rest, which was provided as a social centre for fishermen and others connected with the water. When it ceased to be used for this purpose it became St. Clement's Church Hall and remained such until the new hall was built in Rectory Grove in 1924. The gentleman in the foreground looking towards us is Mr. Arthur Cotgrove, a well known character in his time.

93. Elm Road with Pall Mall on the right. It was originally quite literally Elm Road with a thick avenue of elm trees all the way to London Road. Station Road was a later addition. Note the old fashioned milk cart and the entire absence of traffic.

94. Leigh Heath Farm. This farmhouse stood on the London Road just to the east of the flats, Leigh Heath Court, though they did not exist in those days. In fact Leigh Heath Farm was the only building between Lapwater Hall and the boundary with Hadleigh. In our picture the London Road ran across just beyond the trees. The eastern side of the house is shown here. It was probably an 18th century building on the site of a much earlier one. The name of this farm was used at least as early as the 16th century. (P. H. Reaney, Essex Place-names gives 1534 as the first documentary reference to the name.)

95.   Lapwater Hall. This was a red brick farmhouse of the 18th century, though perhaps it was earlier in origin.
Lapwater Court in the London Road now occupies the site of the old house, which survived, though derelict
until the 1950s. It was by no means unattractive and nowadays it might well have been classified as a listed building. Its interest, perhaps even notoriety, has been created by its name. 'The Legend of Lapwater Hall' was published in the June number of Macmillan's Magazine (pp. 108-115) in 1892. Briefly, about 1750 the house stood
empty and it was purchased in a poor condition by one who called himself Gilbert or Gabriel Craddock. He
arrived at Leigh on horseback, but the horse had no ears. He employed local labour to restore the place and as
he planned to be married in May of that year, 1751, he wanted the work done fairly quickly. Craddock frequently visited Leigh and made friends with the Rector, Roger Price, and with Captain Thomas Little who lived at
Eden Lodge. However, Craddock was very parsimonious and limited the amount of beer the workmen on the
house were to receive. In reply to their protests he said 'Go to the pond and lap water'. The local people began
to call the place Lapwater Hall. Late one night Craddock arrived at the house wounded with a gunshot wound
and hid himself away in an old culvert. He was being pursued by Bow Street Runners who wanted him as a
notorious highwayman on the London to Colchester Road named Jerry or Cutter Lynch. In the morning they
found him dead. How much of the story is true and how much is false would make an interesting project for
anyone interested in historical research. The present writer is open-minded on the subject. There is no old
reference to the place as Lapwater Hall. P. H. Reaney gives 1770 as the first documentary reference to Lapwater Hall. The author is indebted to Miss May Foster who lent him a manuscript copy of the Legend of Lapwater Hall.

96. Turnpike Cottage in London Road. This was immediately opposite Westleigh Schools on the corner of London Road and Eastwood Road. It seems that part of London Road was a toll road and the keeper lived here. However, the cottage is not marked on the 1845 map, but in the census of 1851 Maria Hymas of Turnpike House is described as Toll Collector. If this was the turnpike house referred to we can assign a date to it between 1845 and 1851. The children at the cottage gate are Jim, Maud and Olga Nay. The girls are now Mrs. Padgham and Mrs. Bliss who still live in Leigh. The cottage was demolished many years ago. (Benton, p. 331, writing in 1867 calls this Turner's Corner and mentions that tolls were collected on the road here.)

97. The Bridge where Eastwood Road crosses the Prittle Brook. This was taken towards the end of the last century while Belfairs (now the Golf Course) was farm land or woodland, and the brook had not been concreted and ruined pictorially. The bridge was the subject of a legal action at the Quarter Sessions in 1594 and again in 1603 when the Leigh people got into trouble for not keeping it in repair. It was called Sallom Brook Bridge. In 1603 the request was 'for to make Sallom Broke that leadeth from Esswood to Lee for that it is a noysom brydge that neither footmen nor horsemen can pass yf any great water com done'. This was certainly a more beautiful spot when the picture was taken than it is now.

98. Oak Farm (sometimes called Burnt Oak Farm). This was situated in the Leigh Road on the north side, not far from where Leigham Court Drive is now. No architectural descriptions of the building seem to have survived, but from the picture it could be Tudor or earlier. In fact one would not be surprised if the walls were timber framed with wattle and daub fillings.

99. Brickhouse Farm. This was on the site of the present fire station at the corner of Blenheim Chase and Mountdale Gardens. The farm was probably of 18th century date with modern additions. The ancient boundary between Leigh and Prittlewell parishes went through the house and there used to be a line cut in the kitchen mantel piece to show exactly where the boundary passed. (Reaney, Essex Placenames, gives 1777 as the first use of the name Brickhouse Farm. Other farms have as their first recorded dates: Belfairs (from Alan Belenfent, an early owner) 1234, and Gowles Farm, 1504.)

XIV THE LEIGH MARINERS

For about two centuries—the 16th and the 17th—Leigh was famous for its mariners who sailed the seas of the then known world, engaged in trading and perhaps privateering. Some were associated with Trinity House—the body responsible for pilots and aids to navigation round our shores. A number of Leigh mariners became Masters of Trinity House (an honour nowadays held by a personality of national importance); others were brethren. In the later period the Leigh mariners figured prominently in the Royal Navy.

Ships were small in those days, and there seems to have been a thriving ship building industry in Leigh in Elizabethan times, but as larger vessels became the vogue, and perhaps because Leigh Creek was silted up, the place declined as a port and place for ship building.

Whole Leigh families for several generations were mariners. There were the Haddocks, the Salmons, the Goodlads, the Bundockes, the Chesters, the Moyers and others. Judging by their wills some of them made a good thing out of it. Unfortunately they just disappeared from Leigh leaving little trace behind them. Also virtually all the families died out leaving few sure descendants, often none in the male line. It is uncertain if the greatest Leigh mariner family of all—the Haddocks—have left any descendants in the male line, though some in America make the claim.[1]

Apart from their tombs in St. Clement's or the churchyard there are practically no relics of the mariners in Leigh or elsewhere, and even the memorials at the church have suffered some destruction or are in a bad condition, and in some cases hard to identify.

With possibly one exception—the old Custom House—all the houses in which the mariners are known to have lived have been destroyed. It is possible that the Custom House was once a mariner's residence.

Thus the author has little of a visual character to offer in this book under the heading of Leigh mariners, simply because it does not exist. The little that does exist, however, is of interest, and we are printing illustrations that can easily be seen locally.

Notes
1. The Leigh Mariner family of Hare have undoubtedly left descendants in the male line. Francis Hare, Bishop of Chichester (1731-1740) was of the family, and the present family of Hare, formerly of Hurstmonceux Castle, are descended from them. (See Burke's Landed Gentry). Samuel Hare occupied a large house in Leigh in 1671 (Hearth Tax Rolls).

100.   Brasses to the Haddock family in St. Clement's. The pair on the right are Richard Haddock (died 1453) and Christina his wife, while underneath are their children, seven sons and three daughters. The pair on the left are John Haddock, their son, and Alice his wife, while underneath are their children, eight sons and three daughters. These are not the earliest Haddocks living in Leigh as there was a John Haddock who at his death in 1327 owned a house and land.

VNDERNEATH THIS STONE LYETH BVRYED THE BODY OF RICHARD CHESTER OF THIS
PARISH MARINER WHO WHILEST HE LIVED WAS ONE OF THE ELDER BROTHERS OF THE
TRINITY HOUSE AND WAS MASTER OF THE SAID SOCIETY IN THE YERE OF OVR LORD 1615
HE LIVED IN MARRIAGE WITH ELIZABETH HIS WIFE ABOVT 9 YEERES BY WHOM HE HAD
ISSVE 4 SONNS AND ONE DAVGHTER OF WHICH NVMBER ONLY GEORGE AND ROBERT
CHESTER HIS SONNS AND ELIZABETH HIS DAVGHTER SVRVIVED HIM   HE DECEASSED THE
5TH DAY OF APRILL 1632 AND HIS SAID TWO SONNS GEORGE + ROBERT PLACED THIS STONE
HERE IN REMEMBRANCE OF THEIRE SAIDE DECEASSED FATHER

101.   Brass to the Chesters in St. Clement's. The brass depicts Richard Chester
(who died in 1632) and Elizabeth his wife. Their four sons and one daughter are
underneath. Only two sons, George and Robert, with the daughter Elizabeth survived him. Richard Chester was Master of Trinity House in 1615, previous to
being one of the elder brethren. He appears to have lived in two Leigh houses at
different times (unless there were two Richard Chesters in Leigh at that time).
The one was Eden Lodge, the other was the house on the east side of the Strand,
both of which are pictured in this volume, plates 15 and 34. Neither house exists
now though there are still a few folk who can remember Eden Lodge and many
who remember the house on the Strand. The Chester family left Leigh before
1662, and probably the sons of Richard and Elizabeth did not live in Leigh after
their parents' death. There were no Chesters in Leigh after the Hearth Tax Rolls
were made in 1661/2.

102. The Chester Steeple Cup. In Richard Chester's will there is a clause 'I give and bequeath to the Master and Assistants of the Trinity House of Deptford Strand and their successors one gilten cupp to weigh twentie ounces to remain as my gift to the said house for ever'. (proved April 1633). The very handsome and extremely valuable cup was duly given and it still exists, but Trinity House disposed of it to the Victoria and Albert Museum where it is on display. The cup with its lid is 17½ inches high and it has the London Hall Mark of 1625-6. It is solid silver gilded, and inscribed 'Mr. Richard Chester his gift being Mayor of ye Corporation in Anno 1615'. The corporation was, of course, Trinity House.

103. Memorial in the church to Robert Salmon (1566-1641). There were members of this mariner family in Leigh from the middle of the 15th century for two hundred years. There used to be a brass in the church dated 1472 to Robert Salmon. Robert, who died in 1591, was Master of Trinity House in 1588, and Robert, the subject of the memorial, occupied that office in 1617. Doctor Peter Salmon (Physician to King Charles I) was living in Leigh in 1671. (Hearth Tax Rolls 1661/2, and 1671.) He was probably the last in the male line to do so. The inscription on Robert's memorial is in Latin, followed by an English rendering which we reproduce: 'To ye Memory of ye Right Worthy & Worll Robert Salmon Esquire that great instrument of God's Glory & ye Commonwealths Good Restorer of Navigation almost lost 1614. Mr. of ye Trinity House 1617 & ye Glory of it 24 years. Chosen Sheriff of London 1640 whom solid Judgment acute Witt, Uprightnes to all, true piety to God require Admiration & Imitation. Hee died to ye loss of all but his great Comfort June 18 1641 in his 74th year. Was interred with his Ancestors of about 300 years Continuance in ye grave of his Father in this Chancell where he expecteth a Joyfull Resurrection. Doe (Marble stone) preserve his name & bee ye treasurer of his fame But if thou fail his name will bee A lasteing monument to thee.' Robert married Martha Andrewes, sister of Lancelot Andrewes, Bishop of Winchester. There are certainly descendants of Robert and Martha in the female line now living. They are descendants of Jane Salmon, great granddaughter of Robert who married Captain Wm. Morrice, R.N.

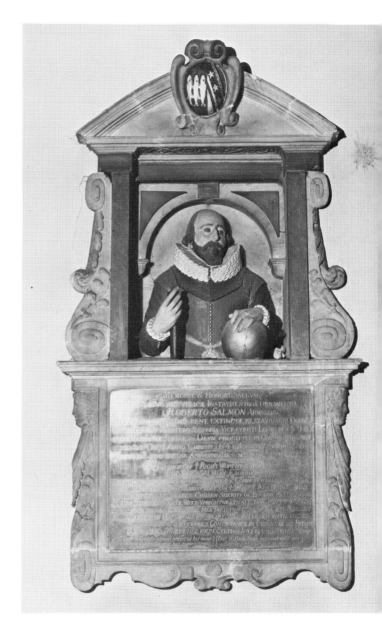

104. (*opposite*) Admiral Nicholas Haddock. The zenith of Leigh maritime fame came with the two greatest of the Haddocks, Sir Richard and his son Nicholas, in the 17th and early 18th century, though they were not much longer to stay in Leigh. The family produced two admirals and an almost uncountable number of naval captains. Admiral Sir Richard (1629-1715) played an important part in the wars against the Dutch following the Restoration of Charles II. He ultimately became Comptroller of the Navy and Admiral of the Fleet by 1690. His son, Nicholas (1685-1746) also had a distinguished career in the navy, reaching the rank of Admiral of the Blue. Both Nicholas and his father were born in the family house at the foot of Billet Lane. Unfortunately no picture of their house has come down to us. They had now risen too high for continuing in such a humble family home and in 1707 Sir Richard sold it. Admiral Nicholas Haddock also felt he belonged to the country gentry so he purchased Wrotham Place in Kent for his own residence. The picture is a reproduction of his portrait in the Maritime Museum at Greenwich.

105. (*top right*) Jane Salmon, great granddaughter of the celebrated Robert Salmon portrayed in plate number 103. He had a son Robert, and he too had a son of the same name who was Jane's father. Both these younger Roberts were mariners, but as their prosperity increased they forsook Leigh and the family became established at South Ockendon. Jane was married to Captain William Morrice R.N. and many of their descendants remain until now, though none are in Leigh. Our picture is a photograph of a portrait in oils now in the Museum of Fine Arts, Richmond, Virginia, U.S.A. Jane's exact date of birth is unknown. It was probably about 1650. She died 1705 and was buried at Deptford.

106. (*bottom right*) Margaret Salmon, another great granddaughter of the famous Robert Salmon. She was sister to Jane and was born in 1654. She married Peter Dare, a mariner of Limehouse (Ratcliffe), which was a smart quarter in those days. He died in 1682 and she then married Robert Castell, a ship builder, of Deptford. She died without any issue in 1715 and was buried at Deptford.

107. Francis Hare, Bishop of Chichester (1671–1740). One of the most prominent mariner families of Leigh during the 16th and 17th centuries were the Hares. The first recorded member was Captain Thomas Hare who died in 1572. They have descendants living now, though not in Leigh. Major T. R. Mordaunt-Hare, M.C. of Teffont Magna in Wiltshire, the senior descendant, gave the author much information about the history of his family.

The best known historically is Francis Hare, Bishop of St. Asaph (1727–1731), then of Chichester (1731–1740). He was not a native of Leigh, but there is little doubt that his father Richard (b. 1636) was. During the bishop's youth the Hares were still living at Leigh.

Francis was educated at Eton and King's College, Cambridge, where in 1708 he became a Doctor of Divinity. In 1700 he was Moderator of the University, and in 1704 was appointed Chaplain General of the Army in Flanders. This marked the beginning of his career as a dignitary of the Church, for in 1707 he was made a Prebendary of St. Paul's (then a paid office which he kept until his death) and residentiary Canon. Queen Anne made him one of her chaplains. In 1715 he became Dean of Worcester and from 1717 Rector of Barnes. He followed the usual, but corrupt, practice of holding many offices in plurality. But in 1727 he exchanged the Deanery of Worcester for the far more lucrative Deanery of St. Paul's, which again he kept until his death.

The Bishop was twice married, first to Bethaia Naylor, heiress of Hurstmonceux Castle, then to Mary Margaret Alston, eldest daughter of John Alston, who ultimately brought with her the estate of the Vaches at Chalfont St. Giles. This became the Bishop's principal residence until his death.

Sir Robert Walpole, whom the Bishop tutored at Cambridge, tried to get him the see of Canterbury when it fell vacant in 1736, but as Francis had opposed the government on a certain issue in the House of Lords he was rejected.

As the Bishop could not have spent much time either in his diocese or at St. Paul's, his career can only be justified on his very profound learning and the theological and biblical writings showing his knowledge of the Classics and of the Hebrew Bible to which he wrote a commentary.

The Bishop was buried in a most unpretentious vault at Chalfont St. Giles Church where a humble mural tablet records his name and those of nine other later members of the family.

Hakluyt in his Voyages (Vol. VIII pp.21–26) mentions Captain Steven (Stephen) Hare of Leigh as Master of the ship 'Mimion' in 1580–81, and on p. 238 as Master of the 'Content' in 1587–88. Other Hares of Leigh in Elizabeth I's time were Samuel, John and Richard.

The family was still in Leigh in the latter half of the next century for the Hearth Tax Rolls for 1668 and 1675 record Samuel Hare Esq. in a house with 12 hearths—the largest in Leigh, but its location is unidentified. Widow Hare had an empty house with 11 hearths (probably the same one) in 1661-62. Richard had a house with two hearths in 1661.

The Church Burial Registers record that Ann Hare was buried in 1691 and Catherine and Mary in 1693. Samuel Hare was buried in the chancel in 1695/6.

Two of the mural tablets destroyed in or before the Victorian restoration were to Katherine Hare (1668), wife of Richard Hare, and Jane, daughter of Samuel Hare (d. 1667, in infancy).

Our photograph of the Bishop is a copy of a miniature belonging to Major Mordaunt-Hare, the only representation of him known to exist.

XV INDUSTRY AND THE SEA

Until our development as a commuter town **Leigh** had depended largely on the sea for its industry, and almost the whole population was dependent, directly or indirectly, on the sea for their livelihood. For perhaps rather more than two centuries (16th and 17th) many Leigh men were mariners who sailed to distant parts. We have always had our fishermen and until recently a good deal of merchandise has been transported by sea to and from Leigh. The five bordari mentioned in the Domesday Book as without land were probably fishermen. However, compared with Victorian times the number of Leigh fishermen is now very small. The 1851 census lists 225 fishermen and fisherlads out of a total male population of 692.

The kind of fishing and the varieties of fish the men have gone out to catch has varied over the years. Shrimps, cockles and whitebait have been prominent in recent generations, but at one time there was a considerable oyster fishery off Leigh.

Now there are only about eight cockle boats working, eight whitebait boats working in pairs and three regular shrimpers.

Pictures of fishing in old times are hard to find and probably do not exist in large numbers, while it is not the policy of this book to portray the present. We show some bawleys that used sails before the internal combustion engine came and displaced the sail.

Many barges used to come into Leigh until fairly recently. We show some pictures of these.

108. View of the Thames off Leigh. This etching is by Edmund Worlledge, and it tells us the kind of craft we should have seen in the estuary about 1843. The rigging of some of the boats is quite different from any that even the oldest Leigh people can remember.

109. The net goes overboard. This picture and the next were published with others on shrimping in the Illustrated London News (July 28, 1883). They were lent to the author by Mrs. A. K. Read (née Emery). The bawley is smaller than the later type and has no winch for hauling in the net. Mr. George Emery was the first of the shrimpers to install a copper on board and cook the shrimps at sea. Until then they were cooked in boilers on the shore. The 1851 census gives the names of some ladies whose occupation was 'shrimp boiler' (Mary Noakes and Eleanor Frost).

110. Shrimpers at work. These bawleys all have their nets down. As they trawled slowly they had to regulate the amount of sail exposed to the wind. When they were out fishing they always towed a punt, (also called a skiff) used for getting to and from the place where the bawley was moored (either in the Ray or, at spring tides, nearer the shore on the flats). In case of emergency or if the net was fouled the punt came into use. The earlier bawleys were smaller than the later, more developed craft, and like the peter boats and pinkies before them in the last century were too small to be able to tow a punt or even to find it necessary.

111. The bawley 'Helen and Violet'. She was owned by Arthur Felton and won the bawley race in the Leigh regatta in three successive years, 1921, 1922 and 1923. The Leigh bawley was a craft first used about the middle of the last century. The later ones were about 35 feet long. They were higher in the bows than at the stern and had a fairly broad beam. They drew 5 feet of water and for that reason they were left moored in the Ray when not in use if the tides were neap, but came close in shore during the spring tides. The bawley's rig was uncommon in that the mainsail had a gaff but no boom—no doubt so that it could be easily brailed up when fishing or the net was being hauled in. They had a topmast and set a large topsail. The bowsprit was long and they used to set a foresail and jib. When extra speed was needed they set a big jib and jib-topsail. Arthur Felton's 'Helen and Violet' was built by J. H. Cann of Harwich. She was not racing in the picture as she is towing her punt. The normal crew was a skipper and mate, but this photograph must have been taken on a special occasion when there were six or more on board.

112. Two bawleys at the end of the race. In another regatta (1906) 'Elsie and Mildred', owned by 'Grannie' Cotgrove narrowly beat Fred Tomlin's 'Erato'. Actually the winner is the boat on the left, as they altered their positions after passing the winning line. Here you can see the great size of 'Erato's' sails. At the beginning of the century there were almost a hundred Leigh bawleys and even up to the 1930s there were probably seventy. No one who did not see the sight could imagine the sheer beauty of the scene in the estuary when this fleet of boats sailed in on the afternoon spring tide. Alas, we shall never see it again. Successive owners of 'Erato' were Fred Tomlin, George Wilder and Cecil Osborne who supplied the author with the pictures.

113. The barges. Much heavy freight was brought into Leigh or taken away by sailing barges. Sand and ballast, bricks, lime, cement, coal and other heavy materials and also grain and hay were carried. Often you could see a barge loaded with hay part of the way up the mast. In fact the barge 'Thomas' owned by Jim Gibbons of Benfleet capsized off Leigh following heavy rain which soaked in and made the load unstable. The barges used Bell Wharf, Victoria Wharf, Theobald's Wharf and when we had the old gasworks there was a wharf for coal at that point. This picture is a typical scene at the Bell Wharf.

114. The barge 'Veronica'. She was said to be one of the last Thames barges working entirely with sail and without an engine. Notice the lee-board at the side of the vessel which was put down when sailing close to the wind. The mainsail is held up by a sprit without gaff or boom.

115. The Thames Jubilee Barge Race 1964.

116. (*right*) Mr. Bob Johnson. He was one of the best known of the Leigh fishing folk. Born in 1839, he died in 1925.

117. (*below*) A group of Leigh fishermen, early this century. From the left: 1. George Turnnidge; 2. ? Tomlin; 3. Tom Emery; 4. George Emery; 5. Fred Emery; 6. 'Padget' Osborne; 7. 'Swedie' Johnson; 8. Reg Turnnidge; 9 & 10 unidentified. At this time the sailmaker's shop was worked by Mr. Angier who had come from Brightlingsea. Mr. Francie Turnnidge followed him about 1902.

118. (*above*) Four Leigh fishermen. From the left: William Johnson, Bob Deal, ? , 'Gully' Wilder.

119. (*right*) Net making. In the old town of Leigh—as in many towns and villages—there were some cottage industries. As a fishing town Leigh had its own including net making and shrimp boiling. The 1851 census lists as net makers Eliza Shaw, aged 25, wife of Thomas Shaw, fisherman, and Charlotte Frost, aged 25, daughter of Isabel Frost, a fisherman's widow. The lady in the picture is thought to be Mrs. Shaw in her later years.

120.   George Kirby. This well known
fisherman was born in 1838 and died in
1910. He is depicted here mending a
peter net. This type of net was commonly
used in Leigh years ago. It was placed in a
gut (the colloquial name for creek) at low
water, and held fast by stakes. The tide
came up and fish were prevented from
passing it during the ebb. At low water
the fishermen came and took their catch.
(See Hervey Benham, 'Once upon a Tide',
for illustration of a peter net. Also see
James Murie's MSS in Southend Central
Library.)

121.   Mr. Joe Deal. He died at the age
of 81 in 1913 leaving (according to a
local newspaper report) one hundred
descendants. He was a well known
Leigh fishing character.

XVI THE LEIGH POTTERY

During the 19th century there was a pottery in Leigh, situated east of the site of the present Grand Hotel and south of Leigh Road, on the rectangular piece of land bounded by what are now Victor Drive and Leighcliff Road, though some of the clay was dug south of Victor Drive. Actually most of the pottery site was in the parish of Prittlewell, the boundary between the parishes passing through or near Wallis's supermarket in a north-south direction.

The owner for many years was David Montague who lived at Leigh House. The little factory produced bricks, tiles, chimney pots, drain pipes and flower pots as well as stone jars and bottles. A certain amount of finer, ornamental items were produced, though they never reached a very high artistic standard; in fact they were rather coarse ware. Some of these pieces are still in the possession of old Leigh families.

The pottery buildings were approached by a narrow country road which is now the Broadway. Some of the clay was dug in the vicinity. Pictures of ponds caused by the digging still remain. The finer white clay needed for some of the products was imported by sea to one of the wharves. Mr. Montague rented the Victoria Wharf at one time. Some of the heavier products were loaded on to barges at Chalkwell beach (close to the present Chalkwell station).

The number of men employed at the pottery was probably from two to three dozen. The returns for Leigh in the 1851 census, in addition to Mr. Montague, list 10 names of males who appear to have been employed at the pottery. Seven were described as potters, four of whom were under 21, two were tile makers, and there was one kiln burner who might have been employed on the lime kiln on Victoria Wharf. Only three of the 10 were natives of Leigh. They were George Rand, Robert Robinson and George Wright. Two came from Lambeth where there was a large pottery. They were William Winter and George Hatlam, while Edward Grant was a native of Battersea.

In addition there were 16 cottages (two rows of eight) in the pottery site but in the parish of Prittlewell where no doubt more employees lived.

The last firing of the kiln took place in 1899, after which the industry came to an end and the site was sold for development. Some of the cottages survived in a broken down condition until fairly recently. There was nothing in them worth printing pictorially.

122.   The Pottery. This was probably taken from the north west of the buildings. Some of the cottages remained until comparatively recently, long after the larger buildings had gone.

123.   The Pottery kiln. This conical kiln was conspicuous from all directions for a long distance. A kiln of this size must have been used for baking the larger and coarser products, the bricks, pipes and tiles.

124. The Pottery pond. Some of the coarser clay used for bricks, chimney pots and tiles had been dug from here. Later it became the water supply for some of the processes.

125. Ornamental Leigh pottery. Some ornamental pieces belonging to Mrs. I. K. Thornton. Most of them have a rough sandy finish, only the flowers and leaves being glazed. This kind of work was only a side line at the pottery. Probably few of the workers were skilled enough to try and make an artistic object.

126. (*right*) Mr. Huggett at work on a pickle jar. He appears to be using a treddle-driven potter's wheel. There was no mechanisation in those days.

127. (*below*) The finishing-off process. The making of these stone jars became an important part of the work of the Leigh Pottery in its later years when ginger beer became popular. Many of these jars still exist, with the name of the mineral water makers glazed on them. The firms, like the pottery are in most cases extinct.

128.   Boys at work in the Pottery. Some of the Leigh youths found employment in the Pottery. As this picture was taken in the 1890s it is scarcely possible that any of them are alive today. Relatives and friends might be able to identify some of them.

XVII SOME 19th CENTURY LEIGH CHARACTERS

This section is in no way a complete biographical description of all Leigh people of the period. It is a mere selection of some well known Leigh people and groups, limited very much by the photographs which the author possesses or to which he has had access. Nevertheless he has tried to make his selection as representative as possible in the circumstances.

In a few cases the photographs were taken in the present century but the people whom they portray were born in the 19th century and some of them very early in that century.

129. Lady Olivia Bernard Sparrow. There is every indication that tenants had occupied the manor house, and that the lords of the manor had been non-resident at any rate for some centuries. This meant that most probably their only interest in Leigh was financial, with little concern for the personal welfare of the ordinary people. In 1805 Lady Sparrow inherited the manor on the death of her husband, Brigadier General Sir Robert Bernard Sparrow of Worlingham in Suffolk. Although there is no evidence that she lived in Leigh she took a great interest in the people. She was instrumental in providing two new supplies of water for the people of the old town, wells on the Strand and near Bell Wharf, in 1832 and 1836 respectively. (Benton, p. 398) She was a deeply religious woman and although an Anglican was an extreme Evangelical, belonging to a group called Recordites. During the latter years of Edward Walter's time as Rector (1808-1837) the Church life of the parish became very neglected, chiefly through his infirmity, and the morality of the people was said to be of a low order. Lady Sparrow according invited a very effective evangelist to come and raise the spiritual tone of the people. He was the Rev. Ridley Herschell, to whom we devote a later section. The same motive inspired Lady Olivia to found a school in 1834. It was on the north side of what is now the Broadway, behind the site of the present Woolworths. Lady Sparrow died in 1863, and her heirs had apparently little interest in Leigh, and as the school was not secured by trust it was sold up with the rest of her Leigh assets. Her only son died in 1818 and her daughter, Millicent, who had married the Duke of Manchester, died in 1848. Lady Olivia Sparrow deserves to be remembered as a benefactor of Leigh. Her Christian conscience caused her to divert some of her not inconsiderable personal possessions for the benefit of others and for the common good when generosity of that sort was all too rare.

130. Lady Sparrow's Coat of Arms. This is to be seen in the window of Faith and Hope on the south side of the sanctuary of St. Clement's Church. The left side includes the Sparrow, the Bernard and the St. John arms. The right side is of Acheson (Earl of Gosford) who was her father. No doubt she helped financially in the restoration of the church at this time.

131. Revd. Ridley Herschell. This remarkable man was a Polish Jew born in 1807 at Strzelno (Benton, p. 321). His original first name was Haim, and he was grandson of a Rabbi. He wandered round as a young man, studying and teaching at Berlin University. In Paris he studied the Christian religion and nearly became a Roman Catholic, but he finished up in England where he was baptised by the Bishop of London, taking Ridley as his Christian name. He appears not to have taken holy orders but he became a lay evangelist. In this capacity Lady Sparrow invited him to work in Leigh amongst the inhabitants of the old town. He seems to have used her school and to have worked closely in collaboration with her. He undoubtedly had a great influence on the people in the parish whom the Church at that time was failing to touch. A Jew converted to Christianity in those days would create an attraction, and he converted many. Although he spent under two years in Leigh he made such an impact that 700 people subscribed to give him a Bible and a Prayer Book as a farewell gift. It is noteworthy that his son Farrer Herschell became Lord Chancellor in two of Gladstone's cabinets. He was the first Lord Herschell (DNB).

132. Michael Tomlin. Amongst Ridley Herschell's converts was Michael Tomlin, one of Leigh's most remarkable men in the Victorian period (S. F. Johnson, 'Michael Tomlin', printed privately, but a copy is to be seen at Southend
Central Library). He was born in Leigh in 1814 and lived until 1903. During
Ridley Herschell's campaign he and his lively pals thought they would go to one
of his services 'just to see what a Jew looks like'. There he experienced sud-
den conversion which made a violent change on his whole mode of life. Then-
ceforth he became a Methodist preacher and evangelist, both in the first Methodist Church in the old town, and as an itinerant preacher all over Essex. He
once walked 30 miles each way on a Sunday to preach at Goldhanger. In
Leigh he preached at a small school on Leigh Hill named after Herschell.
(Later it became a 'British School', surviving until well into this century: the
building is still there.) Then he turned his attention to Southend where he
founded a church near the Southend front. As a fisherman he was tremendous-
ly strong and with his mate rowed a punt full of skate up to the Blackwall Market to beat the normal form of transport. The mate collapsed in the process,
but Michael continued and finished the journey alone. He was buried in St.
Clement's churchyard, west of the tower and the grave is marked by a memorial to him.

To the Glory of God and in loving memory of
Robert Eden.
Bishop of Moran, Ross & Caithness, Primus.
Founder of this Cathedral Church.
Born 1809. Died 1886.

This Memorial is erected by his surviving Children, Grandchildren
and Great-Grandchildren.

133. Robert Eden. After the unhappy years that ended Edward Walter's ministry as Rector there was the first of three exceptional Rectors of that century --Robert Eden. He was the son of a north country baronet (the same family as Anthony Eden, Prime Minister and, later, Lord Avon). He arrived as a young priest, and he was strongly influenced by the Tractarian (or Oxford) Movement that was begun by Keble, Newman and Pusey. Dr. Eden did a tremendous amount for Leigh during the 15 years he was here, not only with the church and its services, but in a social capacity. During the cholera epidemic in Leigh in 1849 he went round nursing the victims and massaging them with his own hands. He was chairman of the Rochford Board of Guardians and took a personal interest in the poor of Leigh (Bride, pp. 43, 46, 51, 53). He was a wealthy man, having been left a substantial estate by a parishioner in a former parish where he had worked. He used his money generously for the public good. A new Rectory was built, of a size fashionable for rectories at that time, but far too big for later needs. It is now the Public Library. Eden restored the church, and perhaps the east and south windows of the chancel, and the poppy-headed pews were introduced at this time. He has sometimes been discredited for his alleged destruction of some of the monuments to earlier worthies in the church and churchyard. Certainly Admiral Nicholas Haddock's exterior monument disappeared about this time, but there is no evidence of anything approaching a wholesale destruction of monuments by Eden. The National Schools on Church Hill were founded by him in 1847. He gave the land, and paid for the cost of the building. It was unfortunate that the steep slope ultimately made the foundations unstable, and, as we have seen, the Church School did not survive. In 1851 Robert Eden was elected Bishop of the Scottish see of Moray Ross and Caithness. He founded Inverness Cathedral and our illustration is his memorial in that cathedral. It is a true likeness of him. (DNB)

134. Robert Eden's Coat of Arms. This is in the same window as Lady Sparrow's arms. On the left is Eden quartered with Smythe of London. On the right is Parke.

135.   Canon Walker King. Robert Eden was followed as Rector by two clergy who did not stay long.
Christopher Harrison remained from 1852 until 1855, and little is remembered of him. Frederick Murray
followed and held the benefice until 1859. He was son of the Bishop of Rochester (Leigh was in the
Rochester diocese then). He was also a kinsman of the Duke of Athole. Little is remembered of his ministry.
Walker King followed and remained until his death in 1892. He was grandson of a previous Bishop of
Rochester, and brother of Edward King, the saintly Bishop of Lincoln. Walker King was an oarsman when
at Oriel College, Oxford. In 1847 there was no proper Oxford and Cambridge boat race at Putney owing to
a dispute over the conditions under which it was to be rowed. However both the Oxford and Cambridge
crews entered for the Grand Challenge Cup at Henley Regatta, King being one of the Oxford crew. Not only
did Oxford beat Cambridge, but they went on to win the Grand Challenge Cup. Unfortunately because of
the unusual circumstances no blues were awarded that year. (The author obtained this information from Mr.
J. L. Kenny, Secretary of Oriel College Boat Club, who consulted Oxford Rowing (Rev. W. E. Sherwood)
and Record of the University Boat Race 1829-1883 (G. Treherne & J. Goldie).) Walker King raised the religious life of Leigh to a high level, and brought to St. Clement's the zeal and devotion that had come to the
Oxford of his time with the Tractarian movement. More than this, his pastoral interest penetrated every
sphere of the life of Leigh parish, and he became its natural leader. He cared for all his people and had a
sensitive social conscience in days of poverty and much suffering. It is said that he gave a large proportion
of the emoluments of the benefice to worthy objects in Leigh and the relief of the needy, himself having
some private means. Walker King, who became a Canon of St. Albans and the Rural Dean of Rochford
Deanery, was greatly loved by the Leigh people. They had a high regard for his family and were interested
in their doings. His unmarried brother, Edward, was Professor of Pastoral Theology at Oxford, and from
1886 Bishop of Lincoln. He was a not infrequent visitor to Leigh and was loved by many Leigh people. In
1872 the Rector inaugurated the scheme whereby the chancel was lengthened, and at Christmas in that
year the choir wore cassocks and surplices for the first time. By now there were daily services in the church.
The Canon's death in 1892 was greatly lamented by all Leigh. It is recorded that the Leigh fishing fleet,
spending the summer based at Harwich, all flew flags at half-mast on receiving the news of his passing, so
much had he done for their welfare. The picture shows Canon and Mrs. King with their three daughters and
Mr. Bert Robinson, who was for many years in their household.

136. The Bishop at the Rectory. Bishop Edward King of Lincoln (1829-1910) was one of the most revered bishops the Church of England has ever produced, recognised for his personal sanctity and great pastoral influence as bishop in the great and almost entirely rural diocese of Lincoln. Being brother of Canon Walter King he took part in the family gatherings and the picture shows us one of these. Back Row: (from left to right) 1. Rev. (later Canon) Robert (son); 2. Mr. Edward (son); 3. Captain Edward Rodd (son-in-law); 4. Canon Walker King; 5. Rev. Henry (son); 6. Mr. Charles (son). Middle Row: (from left to right) 1. The Bishop of Lincoln; 2. Mrs. Walker King; 3. Mrs. Rodd (nee Annie King) with her child Stanhope. Front Row: (left to right) 1. Mrs. Kirton (nee Juliana King); 2. Miss Emily King.

137. Canon King and the Admiral. The small boy is Edward Leigh Stuart King, son of Mr. Charles King and grandson of Canon Walker King. The child sometimes wore a little sailor suit and his grandfather called him 'the little admiral'—a prophecy which could not have been more true. Leigh (as he was always called) entered the Royal Naval College in 1903, was Midshipman in 1905, Sub-Lieutenant in 1908 and rose through every rank of naval officer to become Rear Admiral in 1938, Vice Admiral in 1941, retiring later as Admiral in 1945. His complete biography would take up much space. He served in HMS Repulse during the Prince of Wales' African and South American tours in 1925; Chief-of-Staff to Commander-in-Chief, Home Fleet, 1938 commanded the 15th Cruiser Squadron in 1940 and 1941; Lord Commissioner of the Admiralty 1941-2; Principal Liaison Officer to the Allied Navies 1943-5. He was awarded MVO and CB. In addition he was given orders by Greece, the Netherlands and Belgium. Admiral King was mentioned in Despatches in 1942 for 'outstanding courage, fortitude and resolution during the Battle of Crete'. This was truly a wonderful career for Canon King's 'little admiral'.

138. Canon King sets out to visit his more distant parishioners. The vehicle is standing outside the porch of the old Rectory (now the Library) but in those days the porch was on the east side. When converted into the Library it was transferred to the north side.

139. Canon Robert Stuart King. Canon Walker King was followed by his youngest son who had been or-
dained by his uncle Bishop Edward King in 1889 and served at St. James', Grimsby. He was only 30 on his
appointment to Leigh and he had been curate to his father for a short time before his death. He brought
with him youth and lively vigour besides the teaching and development in worship which followed the
Oxford Movement and soon became characteristic of St. Clement's. He had a commanding and extremely
attractive personality. Being himself a native of Leigh he felt he was a real Leighman, and the Leigh people
thought he was one of them. There was a vigorous church life under his leadership and he kept pace with
the growth of Leigh in enlarging the church by the addition of the south aisle and vestries as well as by
founding the new churches of St. Margaret's and St. James'. He established St. Thomas' Mission in the old
town. Canon Robert King was a great athlete. Four times he played association football for Oxford University, and also gained an English international cap. He brought his football prowess into Leigh, giving
strength to the local team. He was, like his father, very pastorally minded, and ministered to the Leigh
people whether they were regular worshippers or not. During a typhoid epidemic he went into the bed-
rooms of the sufferers and prayed with them when everyone had been warned not to go near. The Canon
took a great interest in local affairs, sitting on the Leigh Urban District Council of which he was chairman
for a time. He strongly opposed amalgamation with the borough of Southend, and when that project materialised he did not seek a place on the borough council, though none was more fitted than he to be a
mayor. There was an anxious time for the cockle industry when officials alleged that Leigh cockles were
polluted. The Rector played a leading part in the cocklers' defence during the court proceedings, and made
hay of the opposing counsel while he was being cross examined. So the cocklers won the day. His death in
1950 brought to an end the 90 years in which two great Canon Kings had been Rector, and it was indeed
the end of an era.

140. Canon R. S. King as the footballer with two members of the Leigh team.

141. (below) Leigh Rectory Yard Football Team. When Canon King was approaching his fifties some of the youths of Leigh used to play football with the Rector in the Rectory yard (now covered by Broadway West). They used improvised goals. Then they had the bright idea of forming a proper team and playing in local competitions. They registered with the Essex Football Association as Leigh Rectory Yard. Some difficulties arose about accepting a team with such a name. The officials thought it was a joke, but in the end they gave way and the Leigh Rectory Yard F.C. became a reality. To the surprise of all they won the Essex Junior Cup. Canon King is seated in the middle, wearing a cap.

142. Rev. William Heygate. This member of a well known Southend family was curate of the parish from 1857 until 1869. He was a prolific writer of religious books as well as being author of a book of local anecdotes. He was liked by the Leigh people and himself paid for the re-pointing of the exterior of the church.

143. Rev. H. S. Nichol was curate of Leigh from 1892 until 1895. At Cambridge he was awarded his cricket blue and kept wicket for the Cambridge XI.

144. William Foster 1817-1900. Though not a native of Leigh William Foster came here at an early age. He was landlord of the King's Head and was also a coal merchant. In the 1850s he built, and lived in, Pittington House in New Road. He held every office in the town except that of churchwarden. For 30 years he was a Guardian of the Poor, and when Rochford Rural District Council was formed he was elected to represent Leigh. He was head of the poll at the first election to Leigh Parish Council, and was its first chairman. He was for many years, an Overseer and surveyor of roads. At one time he owned the Ray and was involved successfully in a law suit over it. He gave to St. Clement's church a window in the south aisle in memory of his wife. Mr. Foster was chiefly instrumental in bringing gas lighting to Leigh and in introducing street lighting by gas. He was principal shareholder in the new gas company. He was awarded the Royal Humane Society's medal for life saving from drowning.

145. Henry William King, 1816-1893. This outstanding man, with strong Leigh connections, was one of the pioneers of antiquarian and archaeological researches in Essex when the romantic movement drew interest in that direction during the last century. He was the son of W. H. King, collector of customs at the port of Leigh. He was an official in the Bank of England and he spent all his spare time and his vacations visiting churches and other ancient buildings or delving into old manuscripts that nobody had seen, perhaps for centuries. His knowledge of Church and manorial matters was tremendous, and he was blessed both with a retentive memory and a skill for making sketches of old features in buildings. King published much in learned magazines and journals, but left no great published work. However, his great work, in five manuscript folio volumes entitled Ecclesiae Essexiensis, is in the Essex Record Office, with other of his works. He laboriously transcribed the Leigh Manor Records and the work is at the Southend Central Library. He was a founder member of the Essex Archaeological Society and for a long while was its secretary. The Leigh people nicknamed him 'Antiquary' King. He was a keen churchman and strongly supported the Catholic trends in the Church of England. The processional crucifix at St. Clement's is in his memory. A long obituary and detailed account of his work and contributions to antiquarian knowledge can be found in Essex Review, January 1894, pp. 19-24.

146. Ben Barnard, 1840-1913. Old Leigh knew him as Uncle Ben. He was a quaint and interesting character with a strong personality. He was prominent in local government and Leigh enterprises in the last century, and in politics he was a fervent liberal. He shone at election times, and in one election his eloquence proclaimed to the listeners at a meeting 'None of the others have any moral right to be elected except the Rector or me, for we are the only born Leighmen'. It went down in Leigh of that time, and he and the Rector topped the poll. He had a terrific flow of language as a public speaker though he had no more education than the local school could give him. He served on the Board of Guardians, and was an Overseer and one of the members of the first Leigh School Board. He was one of the most tender hearted of men with a genial disposition, in fact in the end he suffered as a result of his extreme generosity. A contemporary says of him 'He had a kindly eccentricity of manner which sometimes found expression in a volubility of speech, the speed of his utterances being nothing short of amazing'.

147. Dr. James Murie. In 1888 James Murie arrived in Leigh to reside, and spent the rest of his life as a Leighman until his death, aged 93, in 1925. In his later years an eccentric, he lived alone in a small cottage in New Road. Murie was born in Glasgow, and took an M.S. degree at Glasgow University as well as LL.D. at St. Andrews. He held posts as pathologist to Glasgow Royal Infirmary, lecturer in comparative anatomy at the Middlesex Hospital, assistant conservator to the Royal College of Surgeons and prosector to the Zoological Society of London. In 1861 he was medical officer and naturalist to Speke and Grant's exploration of the River Nile. He made a deep study of the fish of the Thames Estuary. In our picture he is portrayed giving a lecture on this subject.

148.   Alfred Boyton (right), alias Gottie or Ponto. Much has been written about this extraordinary Leigh character. He was big and strong, dominating and quite eccentric, sometimes drunk and quarrelsome, yet there was a likeable side to him. A. E. Copping wrote two books featuring him, 'Gottie and the Gov'nor' and 'Gottie in Furr'n Parts'. He was more often than not walking the streets of old Leigh bare-footed. He often won the walking, or climbing the greasy pole, contests at Leigh Regatta. H. N. Bride relates two incidents in detail which figure Gottie. Once he fell overboard while out shrimping and survived after being 20 minutes under water from which he was fished up in another bawley's net. On another occasion he won a bet that he would load a barge with sand over four tides. However, a well-informed native of Leigh warned the present author that Copping's books, though they make interesting reading, must not be taken as gospel truth. This does not take away the fact that Gottie was an extraordinary man and an interesting Leigh character who deserves to be remembered. He is pictured here with Fred Cotgrove.

149. The Herschell School: a class of girls in the 1890s.

150. New Road Methodist Church: Sunday School Teachers, 1913. Back row: Edith Kemp, ? , ? , Em. Robinson, Frank Bridge (holding his son), Brubs Bridge, Mrs. Bridge, Ben Palmer, Mrs. Tilly Palmer, 'Fidler' Bridge, Ted Cotgrove, Fred Partridge, Charlie Robinson, Wal Cotgrove. 2nd Row: Reg. Cotgrove, Tom Kirby, Frank Bridge (nephew of No. 5 back row), Alice Robinson, Lil Partridge, Nellie Cotgrove, Mrs. Fred Partridge, Mrs. Charlie Robinson, Fanny Cotgrove, Jimmie Axcell, George Bridge, Johnnie Pepper. 3rd Row: Mrs. Bridge (mother of No. 3, 2nd row), Mrs. 'Fidler' Bridge, Mrs. Alice Robinson, Ethel Partridge, Peggy Bridge, Alice Osborne, Pem Osborne, Amy Partridge, Grace Tomlin, May Noakes, Ethel Robinson. Sitting on the grass: Rosa Hart, Olive Noakes holding Flossie Cotgrove, Wally Bridge, Daisy Bridge.

151. Leigh Salvation Army: 1902. By the turn of the century the Salvation Army was established firmly in Leigh, and there was a strong band by 1902. From the left, standing: John Noakes, 'Bibbles' Livermore, Ashman Wilder (Bandmaster), Johnny Johnson, Ned Gisby, H. Thompson, Colour Sergeant Cotgrove, Percy Kirby, Mick Johnson, George Bray, Ted Bradford, Mr. Dix, Eddie Turnnidge. Kneeling: Sam Richie, 'Sweedie' Johnson (drummer), W. Little, G. Thompson. The Ladies, Captain Green, Captain Pillage and Adjutant Prowse. There is no doubt that the Salvation Army touched many men of Leigh at that time where other Christian bodies were failing. A contemporary publication records that two of the band in our picture 'were before conversion, so noted for their boxing encounters and drinking bouts that they were often hauled up before the magistrates charged with drunkenness and riotous conduct; in fact their presence in the street was a menace to the more respectable members of society'.

152. St. Clement's Clergy, Choir and Servers in 1904. From left, back row; Eddie Brewer, ? Ushwright, Arthur Kerry, Sidney Cater, ? Watts (organist), Albert Kerry. Second Row: George Cable, Ken Burgess-Smith (server), Gus Young, Eddie Burgess-Smith (server), Herman Axcell, Bert Burgess-Smith (server), Alf Cotgrove (Hurricane), ? Bromley. Third Row: Arthur Bowen, Arlie Jobling, Arthur Turnnidge, Fred Brewer, Sid. Perry. Fourth Row: Frank Thompson, Cecil Bundock, Edric Brewer, Rev. A. B. Bennett (curate), Rev. R. S. King (Rector), Arthur Cotgrove, Bert Sims, Fred Thompson. Fifth Row: Bert Cotgrove, Leslie Borer, Walker Brewer, George Cotgrove, Albert Cotgrove, Claude Turnnidge, Charlie Collins, Alan Ferguson, Louis Cotgrove, 'Mobbie' Perry, Stanley Chambers. The names were supplied by Mr. Louis Cotgrove.

153. Old Town Methodists: Society Class, 1902. Back Row: Frank Bridge, Henry Johnson, Dick Deal, James Deal. Middle Row: Albert Going, Tom Ritchie, Richard Harvey, William Kemp, Japheth Cotgrove, William Bridge, Tom Robinson, Fred Partridge, Charlie Robinson, Jim Noakes, William Emery. Front Row: Joe Deal, Bob Emery, John Brock, William Oliver, Elijah Risby, Richard Kirby, Daniel Lester, Robert Ford, Pilot Harvey.

154.   The Leigh Town Football Team in the 1890s. Here they are with all the four trophies
they won that year. From the left, back row: ? , 'Ginger' Emery, Jim Axcell, 'Whitehead'
Turnnidge. 2nd row: ? , Charlie Cadman, 'Sonny' Harvey, Archer Noakes (trainer). Front
row: 'Bobber' Deal, 'Proctor' Meddle, ? , Bob Turnnidge, Arthur Felton.

155.   A Leigh Football Team in the 1890s. They were officially known as the Prittlewell Greyhounds though they were really Leigh Town Juniors. Stephen Johnson founded the team to play
in a Southend competition, but they were refused admission because they were not a Leigh team.
They got over the difficulty by meeting in a house just over the boundary and by playing in a
field on the other side. They called themselves the Prittlewell Greyhounds though they were all
Leigh to the fingertips. We can only identify a few of them. Left front: Burder and Meddle;
centre front: Stephen Johnson holding the trophy they won. Back right: Edward Bundock, and
in front of him Walter Bundock.

156. The Leigh Hockey Club, 1907. From left, standing: W. E. O'Brien, Greenwell, F. Bolton. Kneeling: H. S. Coatsworth, Dr. W. D. Watson, (Capt), J. H. Howell. Sitting: H. P. Cooper, W. F. Sargerson, E. F. Thomas, Rev. A. T. Stiff, C. W. Box.

157. The Leigh Fire Brigade, 1909. They are with their new mechanised engine under the command of Captain Johnson (extreme left). Their fire station, now used for other purposes, is on the east side of West Street at the Broadway end.

158. Three generations of a Leigh family. Bob Johnson (1839-1925) on the right. Next to him is his son, Harold, generally called 'Darrell', who was captain of the Leigh Fire Brigade and a member of the former Leigh Urban Council. Next to him is his son, Edwin. On the extreme left is Stephen who was best known in local public affairs. He was on the Leigh Urban Council, and after the amalgamation he was councillor, then alderman and finally Mayor of Southend (November 1945 to May 1949).

159. Christmas is coming. In the days before refrigeration the butchers displayed all the Christmas meat and poultry in the shop front. Mr. E. G. Johnson (often called 'Brownie') had this shop in the Broadway at the corner of Alexandra Road. Here is the display for Christmas 1910. Mr. Johnson's son Cyril is in the middle of the picture. To the right is Harold Tomlin, and to the left Percy Bowen and Alf. Emery.

XVIII MISCELLANEOUS EVENTS DURING THE 19th AND 20th CENTURIES AND OTHER MATTERS OF INTEREST

Leigh Fair

On the second Tuesday of May every year a fair was held in Leigh. It was a privilege granted to the Lord of the Manor in ancient days. Originally fairs were instituted for trading and business purposes, but generations ago in most cases the fairs became occasions of merry making. It was so in Leigh according to those who have heard people of former generations talking about it. There were swings and roundabouts, coconut shies and all forms of amusement that the Victorian period could produce, as well as stalls for the sale of eatables. Part was on the Bell Wharf, part in the market place and wider parts of the High Street as far as the Strand.

The only visual relics of the fair that the author could produce are three fairings, numbers 1, 2 and 3 in the illustration. Number 1 belongs to the author, 2 to Mrs. I. K. Thornton and 3 to Miss Rosemary Thornton. The date of Number 3 is 1861.

The firm who supplied the merry-go-rounds and the rest of the paraphernalia were the Bibby family. Mrs. Bibby was a very big and stately lady and on the Sunday morning before the fair she always appeared in church clad in a black mantel.

Commemoration China

Number 4 on the illustration is a marmalade dish decorated with the badge of the Leigh Urban District Council—a boat in sail imposed on a cockle shell. Number 5 is a ribbon plate eight inches in diameter. There were others with different pictures of Leigh on them.

The Church Garden Fete. From some date in the 1880s the custom arose of having a Garden Fete for church funds in the large Rectory garden and adjoining meadow. The situation, overlooking the estuary, was ideal and the event attracted people from far and wide. The town was involved and not merely the regular worshippers. A tug-of-war between fishermen and landsmen aroused both interest and rivalry. The event went on until 1925 when the Rectory and meadow passed out of the hands of the church.

160.   Garden Fete stall holders and helpers. This was in the early 1890s, just after Canon R. S. King became Rector and while Rev. H. S. Bennett was curate. Some of the readers will be able to recognise their great grandparents and grandparents in this picture.

161.   Garden Fete, 1907. The scene is on the Rectory meadow, now occupied by the two blocks of St. Clement's Court. The building in the rear was the Rectory (now the library).

162. Garden Fete, 1907, the refreshment tent and helpers. Many old Leigh faces are in this picture. Who remembers Arthur Cotgrove, the bearded gentleman on the left? Emily Eaton, the little dwarf, is in the middle of the picture.

163. The Garden Fete, pre-1910. The Leigh Town Band. We were well enlivened by the town band—plenty of bright music and plenty of fortissimo. They were a real Leigh band, including the two churchwardens and all were familiar faces. It did not require uniforms to produce bright music.

164.   Garden Fete, ?1919, the shooting gallery. Dr. Wacher is taking aim while Canon King looks on with great interest. The two boys on the left are the sons of the curate, Rev. A. T. Stiff.

165.   The Garden Fete, 1907, the baby show. The picture speaks for itself. Canon King is seated on the ground in front. The winner was Jack Saunders, seated on his mother's knee third on the right from Canon King.

166.   Leigh's own locomotive. When our railway opened in 1855 the company hired locomotives and rolling stock from the old Eastern Counties Railway. In 1880 we had 12 engines of our own specially designed, and the following year six more were put into service including the one illustrated (No. 14). They were built by the firm of Sharp Stewart. It was the custom of the London Tilbury and Southend Railway to give its engines names as well as numbers. No. 14 was called LEIGH. Slight changes were made during the course of the years, for instance they began with a tall and narrow funnel called a 'stove pipe funnel'. These were replaced by shorter ones of a different shape. Here is LEIGH at the Plaistow shed in 1911. The colour of the LTSR passenger locomotives was a fairly bright green outlined in maroon with an interior vermilion line, and certain parts picked out with other colours. They were indeed very smart and distinctive. When LTSR was taken over by the Midland Railway the green locomotives were immediately painted red, their names taken off and they were given new numbers. Our LEIGH became 2123. Then on amalgamation in 1923 we became part of LMSR and LEIGH became, first, 2213 and, finally 2090. In 1935 she went out of service and probably no longer exists.

167. Leigh Urban Council Offices. In 1897 Leigh civil parish was granted an Urban District Council and it retained this status until the amalgamation with the borough of Southend in 1913. The new urban council needed adequate administrative offices, and these were provided in 1912. The picture shows the opening ceremony. In front of the closed door is Canon King, the Rector, while on his right is Mr. (later Sir) Frederick Senier.

168. Memorial Service for King Edward VII. This was held on 20 May 1910 at St. Clement's. Either it was held in the churchyard to accommodate the large crowd, too large for the church, or the town band under the direction of Mr. W. C. Crooks, the church organist, played suitable music in the churchyard after the service was over. The picture, incidentally, shows the south aisle of St. Clement's in its unfinished condition terminating with a lean-to vestry in corrugated iron.

169 and 170.   High Tide in the High Street. The Thames Estuary has intermittently been visited by exceptionally high tides from which the low lying parts of Leigh have suffered. None have probably ever surpassed the great tides of 31 January/1 February 1953. Here we have pictures of the midday tide on 1 November 1921. The first is at Bell Wharf the second outside the Peter Boat. In the latter people are standing apparently quite comfortably bare footed, even though it was November. That particular day was remarkably fine and warm.

171. A whale comes to Leigh. In 1890 a whale was washed up on to the shore below Leigh and towed into the creek by some fishermen. Benton mentions that in 1806 a 36 foot long whale had come to Leigh and in 1826 one which was 46 feet long. The 1890 whale was hauled up on to the Bell Wharf, presumably to exhibit a curiosity to the people of the town, hoping perhaps that it might also have some commercial value. Oil oozed from it copiously and it slid away. As decomposition set in it became a public nuisance and had eventually to be cut up and buried somewhere in the marshes. The picture shows two fishermen sitting on the unfortunate creature, rather proud of their trophy.

172. When the sea froze. In February 1927 the sea actually froze and ice was left as the tide receded from underneath it. What you see here is not snow but frozen sea.

173.   The 'Renown's' noble end. There is no more appropriate way of ending this book than by recalling
an event which has now passed into history—the part played by Leigh boats in the evacuation of the British
Army from France at Dunkirk in 1940. During that operation the 'Renown', a Leigh boat, was lost. The
following gave their lives: Frank Osborne, Leslie Osborne, Harry Noakes and Harold Graham Porter. The
picture shows the 'Renown' at her moorings off the Billet Wharf after her day's work is done. The ebbing
tide symbolises the passing of old Leigh, and the boat that came to such a noble end points to the former
glory of Leigh and its people. But the tide does not go out for ever. It will flow in again, bringing with it a
future and, we hope, a happy future at present unknown.